Maryellen Kim

Ribbon Girls
wind, weave, twist & tie

DRESS UP
Your Room

SHOW
Team Spirit

CREATE
Pretty Presents

FunStitch
STUDIO
stitch your art out.

Text copyright © 2014 by Maryellen Kim

Photography and artwork copyright © 2014 by C&T Publishing, Inc.

Publisher: Amy Marson

Creative Director: Gailen Runge

Art Director: Kristy Zacharias

Editor: Liz Aneloski

Technical Editors: Alison M. Schmidt and Gailen Runge

Cover/Book Designer: April Mostek

Production Coordinator: Jenny Davis

Production Editor: Joanna Burgarino

Illustrator: Jessica Jenkins

Photo Assistant: Mary Peyton Peppo

Style photography by Nissa Brehmer and **instructional photography** by Diane Pedersen, unless otherwise noted

Published by FunStitch Studio, an imprint of C&T Publishing, Inc.,
P.O. Box 1456, Lafayette, CA 94549

Library of Congress Cataloging-in-Publication Data

Kim, Maryellen, 1970-

 Ribbon girls : wind, weave, twist & tie : dress up your room, show team spirit, create pretty presents / Maryellen Kim.

   pages cm

ISBN 978-1-60705-987-5 (softcover)

1. Ribbon work--Juvenile literature. I. Title.

TT850.5.K534 2014

746--dc23

                    2014024988

Printed in China

10 9 8 7 6 5 4 3 2 1

Dedication

This book is dedicated to my honey, Dave. He's the apple of my eye.

Acknowledgments

My family is my reason for living. My sweet, unwavering husband, Dave, has encouraged every hare-brained creative thought I've ever tossed out. Not one time in the past twenty years has he discouraged me from trying. He has sacrificed time, money, and unfathomable energy to help me achieve my goals. I adore him beyond words.

Our beautiful children are my life. My girl, Balin, and her sparkling eyes; handsome David and his sense of humor; Baby Leo and his mushy cheeks—these darlings fill me up. I feel like the luckiest mommy in the world. I have always put them first, and they have rewarded me endlessly. Children first. Always. You'll never regret it.

Family extends well beyond those I live with everyday: my parents and grandparents, my siblings, loving aunts and uncles, a growing group of cousins, and sweet in-laws. So much health and beauty fill this group. A special light shines on us, and an amazing bond ties us together. When we are close to each other, we are in love. When we are far apart, we know that a huge group of loved ones is just a call away. It is amazingness.

My studio family includes Chrissy, Kim, Dana, Kristin, Suzanne, Linda, Amanda, and Jen. They are the ones who pick up the pieces of my disorganization and follow my lead without (much) question. I am so thankful for them.

Other folks who help me along include dear RVA friends Tasha McKelvey, Kelly McCants, and my Richmond Craft Mafia homies. Special thanks to "Captain Crafty" Carrie Smith, Noelle Grosso, and my Miss B., who all keep me focused.

Roxane, Liz, Alison, and the talented folks at **C&T Publishing,** thank you so much for this opportunity and your expertise. You so totally rock. **And finally, thank you to dear Dana Carey,** who implanted the words "keep going" in my brain years ago. Good advice, Dana. Thank you!

Contents

Introduction

Hello, Crafty Kids! I'm so glad you like to make stuff, too! I've spent my entire life making things. There is not much that can compare with starting a project and then seeing the end product. Sometimes people tell me that they are "not creative," but I believe they just haven't given themselves permission to BE creative!

So I'm giving you permission! I think you'll like the projects I've designed, but you know what would be really cool? If you make them a reflection of you and what you love!

The nice thing about crafting with ribbon is that you can easily turn something you already own into something totally new and super cool with just a bit of glue or stitching. Some of the projects in this book are a little more involved than others, but that doesn't mean they are hard.

Look for the project skill level to help you decide which craft you would like to start with. If you have been crafting for a while, you probably will not find any of these techniques tricky at all. But if you are new to making things, try beginning with projects designated *Skill Level 1: Start Here!* If you are comfortable with scissors and a hot glue gun, move on to *Skill Level 2: Now Try This!* If you are a more experienced crafter, try the *Skill Level 3: You've Been Crafting Awhile!* projects.

If you don't know what a particular supply or technique is, check out the Good-to-Know Glossary (page 124). The pictures and information there will help you figure out what you need.

And remember, if things don't turn out perfectly the very first time, just keep on making more. The more experience you gain, the easier the techniques will become!

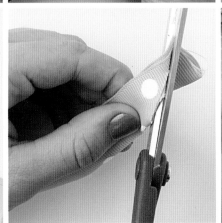

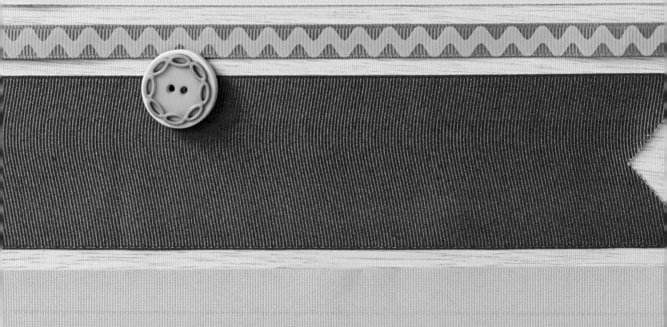

section 1

Style and Embellishment

10

Your Style File

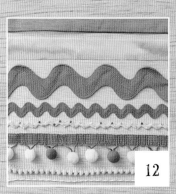

12

All about Ribbons
and Trims

14

Making
Embellishments

Your STYLE file*

We each have a unique style all our own. If you aren't sure what your style is, try making a style file.

All you need is a notebook, sketchbook, some wall space, or even just an old school folder. Start looking through magazines and catalogs. When you see something you like, give it another look and decide what about that image makes it appealing to you.

Is it the color? Is it the texture? Or did a particular element grab your attention, like a bird or flower? Maybe it's a shape or a pattern that you like?

Cut out the image and glue or tape it in your style file. After a while, your file will start to have a "feeling." That feeling is your style! I'm guessing that your favorite color is showing up a lot in that file! Do you love animals? I bet you are seeing a lot of horses and puppies in your style file.

Remember, there is no right or wrong when it comes to creativity! Do what you love, and combine things that make you happy. And don't be afraid of making mistakes. If something doesn't turn out the way you want it to, think about what you can do to turn it into something good. Your style will come shining through!

Hint: I like to use colored pens to make notes in my style file. Sometimes I draw an arrow or jot down a crafty idea, so I don't forget what I had in mind when I chose the image.

All about Ribbons and Trims

Ribbon offers so many ways to be creative! You'll be using ribbon and other trims to create projects that are fun and useful. But first let's talk about some of the different types of ribbon and trim and how you might want to use them.

The ribbons you'll use for the projects in this book are all made of fabric. These aren't the type of curling ribbons used on top of a present, although you *could* use them to make a gift extra special!

Ribbons come in lots of different widths and lengths. At your local craft store, you will find many, many types of ribbon to choose from! They are usually sold on a spool containing between three and ten yards. Some of the projects use A LOT of ribbon, so before you start, make sure you have enough on hand.

Types of Ribbon

A. Grosgrain Ribbon: This ribbon has tiny ridges and lines, which give it a lovely texture. It comes in zillions of colors and is not too stiff. But it is stiff enough to hold its shape very well. It's great for making bows and loopy ribbon flowers.

B. Satin Ribbon: I use this ribbon a lot! It's shiny and soft and very fancy looking. It also holds its shape pretty well but is not quite as stiff as grosgrain.

C. Jacquard Ribbon: This really heavy-weight woven ribbon is great for clothing and belts, and it comes in many beautiful patterns and colors. Most craft stores don't have a huge selection of these ribbons, but they can be ordered online.

D. Wired Ribbon: Some of the previous types of ribbons also come in a wired variety. The fun thing about wire-edged ribbon is that it is very easy to shape and holds its shape very well. The wire can also be pulled out from one side of the ribbon to create a ruffle that you can make into a swirly flower.

E. Silk Ribbon: Silk is very soft and wispy. It does not hold its shape well, but it comes in many beautiful colors and is wonderful for use in ribbon embroidery and for making tiny bows. It is also usually washable on the gentle cycle, so it's a good choice for embellishing clothing.

Types of Trim

F. Rickrack Trim: This trim looks like a wavy zigzag and comes in a variety of colors. You'll find that there are several different widths of this trim, which makes it perfect for lots and lots of different projects.

G. Pompom Trim: Pompom trim is one of my favorites! It is made of a woven tape with fluffy balls hanging down. Like rickrack trim, it also comes in lots of colors and sizes. It works great as an edging element, but I like to use it in unexpected ways, too—like rolling it up to make flowers.

Some other materials that you will use:

H. Baker's twine

I. Yarn

Make Your Own

You can also make your own ribbon! Cut strips of fabric to any width you like and use it just as you would a spool of ribbon. If you don't have fabric on hand, you can cut strips from old T-shirts or other clothes. Or try using other craft supplies as you would a ribbon. You can use yarn, felt, and tulle to make fun bows and flowers!

Hint: Ribbon edges can sometimes fray. Fraying means that the tiny fibers at the end come undone and look fuzzy. A ribbon that frays a lot can come undone completely! To prevent fraying, swipe a tiny, tiny bit of clear nail polish along the edge. If you don't have clear polish, use a bit of school glue. A few products, like Fray Check by Dritz, are specifically made to prevent fraying. You can find these products in the notions department of a craft or fabric store.

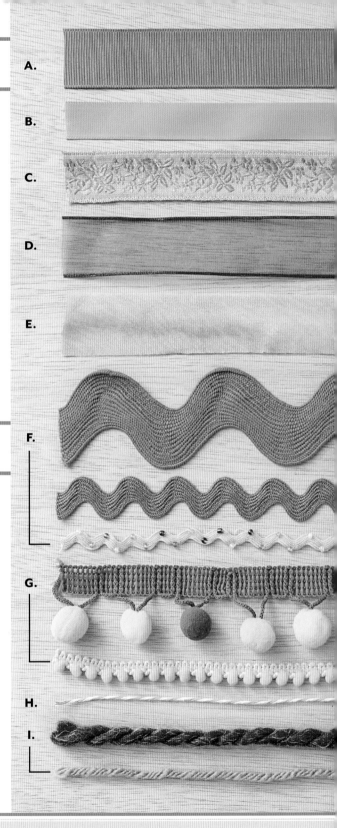

A.

B.

C.

D.

E.

F.

G.

H.

I.

Making Embellishments

Simple Sewing Essentials

Sewing on a Button

1. Cut a length of thread. Thread your needle and tie a knot at the end of the thread.

2. Decide where you want your button to be on your fabric (or whatever you're attaching the button to) and hold it in place. Bring your needle up from underneath, through the fabric, and then through one hole of the button.

3. Pull the thread all the way through until the knot is right up against the fabric, nice and snug.

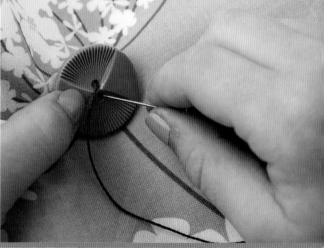

4. Push the needle and thread back through another hole in the button to the back side of the fabric.

(If your button has 4 holes instead of 2 holes, just come up again in another hole, cross your previous stitch, and push the needle and thread to the back again.) I do at least 4 stitches back and forth to make sure my button stays in place for a good long time.

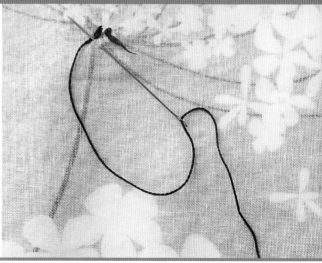

5. Finish by bringing your needle up under the button but not through a hole. Wrap the thread around the button 3 times and then pass the needle back to the underside of the fabric. Make a tiny stitch through the fabric, but not through the button, and tie 2 knots. Trim off any extra thread. There you go! Button attached!

Hand Sewing

Start with a Knot

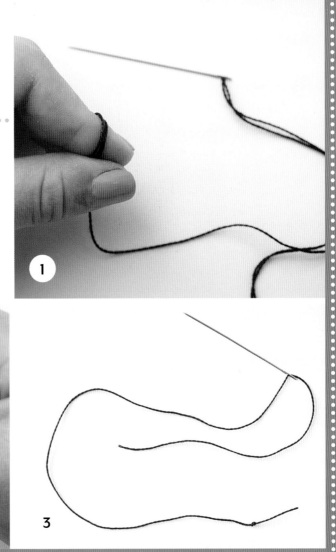

To begin sewing, pass your thread through the eye
of the needle and leave a little tail, as I like to call it.
Wrap the other end of your thread around your index
finger (1). Then roll it off your finger and then pull (2).
You should have a handy little knot, which is quite
important as it will make sure your thread doesn't pull
right through the fabric when you are stitching (3).

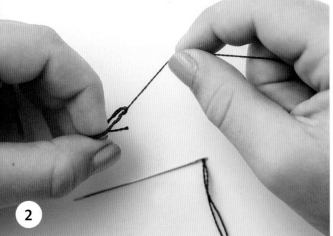

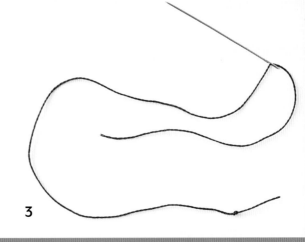

If you will be pulling on your thread a lot (making
gathers, for example), thread the needle, match
up the loose ends of the thread, and knot them
together the same way you did for the single thread.
This is called a double thread. With double thread,
there's no loose end of thread to slip out of the eye
of the needle as you sew.

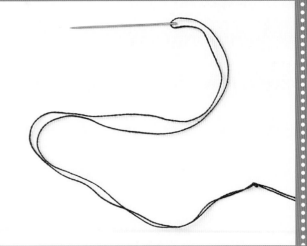

End with a Knot

Just as important as starting your sewing with a knot in your thread is finishing the job with a good knot. You don't want your stitches to pull out or come loose!

End your hand stitching with the needle and thread at the underside of your fabric. I like to do a few tiny stitches back there. Then I make a little loop to push the needle through.

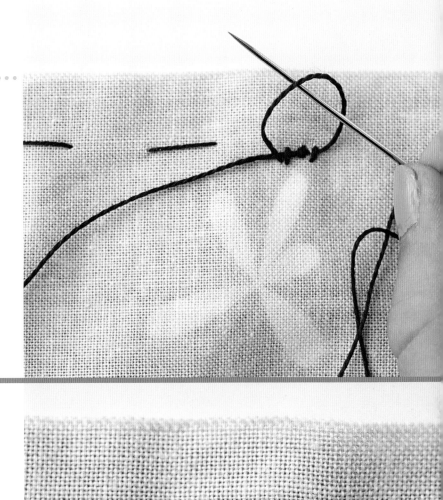

When you push the needle through the loop and pull it tight, you'll have a knot. I suggest doing this one more time to make good and sure your knot won't pull out.

Here's How to Make It Fabulous!

Let's learn how to make some of those pretty bits you can add to your project.

Poppy Flowers (page 20)

Mini Pompom Flower Puffs (page 21)

Satin Ribbon Roses (page 22)

Rickrack Rosettes (page 23)

Loopy Ribbon Flowers (page 24)

Daisy Ribbon Flowers (page 25)

Felt Wind-Up Flowers (page 26)

Notched Felt Fluffs (page 27)

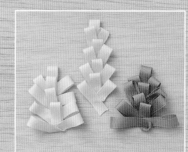
Ribbon Ferns (page 28)

Ribbon Points (page 29)

Ribbon Leaves (page 30)

Pretty Bows (page 31)

Make It Fabulous!

Most of the projects include instructions that encourage you to "Make It Fabulous!" You can follow all the regular instructions and end up with a lovely project. But if you keep going and "Make It Fabulous," you'll see even more of your own personal style shining through.

One way to personalize your projects is to add embellishments. Embellishments add lots of extra-special-ness. Are you a fan of bows or ribbon or glitter? Maybe you like colorful shapes or flowers? Have a look through your style file (Your Style File, page 10) and get inspired. Then use the "Make It Fabulous!" ideas to make your projects as special and one-of-a-kind as you are.

* Add decorative embroidery stitches or use a fun and funky sewing machine stitch, like the zigzag.

* Glue or string beads onto your project.

* Trim the edges of fabrics and ribbons with pinking shears or decorative-edged scissors.

* Attach felt leaves and flowers, buttons, or bows to add more texture to a project.

* Glimmering glitter always makes things extra fancy. Try dipping the edges of your ribbon in glue and then in glitter.

* Layer different widths of ribbon, fabric, or felt on top of each other to add lots of interest to any project.

* Add a cheerful trim of pompons or fringe. You'll turn a darling project into a super-fabulous, most-special project!

You'll need a needle, thread, about 6˝ of ⅝˝-wide ribbon, a button or craft pompoms, and a hot glue gun (page 125) to make a 1½˝-wide flower.

Poppy Flowers

1. Double-thread a needle and knot the ends of the thread together (see Start with a Knot, page 16). Do a loose running stitch along a long edge of the ribbon—start at one end and bring your needle up and down through the ribbon to make stitches ½˝ apart.

2. When you reach the other end of the ribbon, gently pull the thread and slide the ribbon down the thread to form a gathered ruffle.

3. As you push the ribbon all the way down, it will start to curve into a circle. Use the same needle and thread to stitch the short ends of the ribbon ruffle circle together. Make sure to end the stitches on the back of the flower and secure with a small knot.

4. Finish your flower by hot gluing a button or some craft pompoms in the center.

Hint: When you finish a flower embellishment, hot glue a small circle of felt to the back to make it easier to add centers and to provide a smooth background to attach the piece to your project.

You'll need about 11˝ of mini pompom trim, a small scrap of felt, and a hot glue gun (page 125) to make a 1¼˝-wide flower.

Mini Pompom Flower Puffs

1. Begin coiling the trim, keeping the bottom even. Put a dab of hot glue between each layer as the puff begins to form.

2. When you reach the end of the trim, tuck it under the flower and add another dab of hot glue to hold it in place.

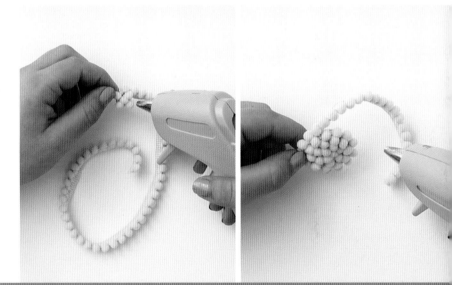

3. Cut a circle of felt to fit the puff. Hot glue the felt to the wrong side of the flower as a backing, if you like.

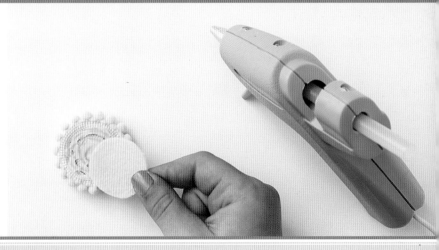

You'll need about 21″ of ⅝″-wide ribbon and a hot glue gun (page 125) to make a flower about 1¼″ wide. These flowers are so pretty, but every time I make them, they look a little different. Yours might be a bit bigger or smaller than the ones here, depending on how tight or loose your twists are. Don't worry! Even if yours have a different look, they will still be fun to make and totally cute!

Satin Ribbon Roses

1. Coil the first 2″ of your ribbon tightly to make the center of your flower. Add a dab of hot glue and start twisting and wrapping the ribbon, putting another dab of hot glue at the bottom of the flower for every 2 or 3 twists.

Hint: Satin ribbon makes a more formal-looking rose with a good bit of shimmer. If you would like a more fanciful flower, try using this technique with a grosgrain ribbon or rickrack. Using different materials will give this flower a very different look!

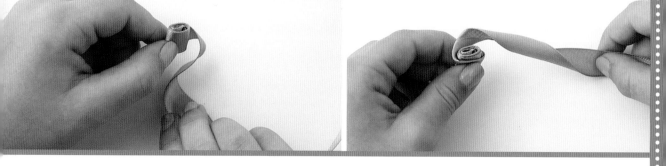

2. Continue twisting, wrapping, and hot gluing until you only have about ½″ of ribbon left. Tuck the end under the flower and hot glue it in place. Done!

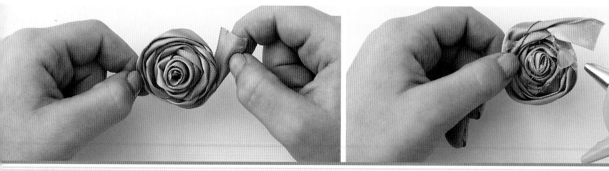

You'll need about 20˝ of rickrack trim, a small scrap of felt, and a hot glue gun (page 125) to make a 1˝-wide rosette. Rickrack trim comes in several different sizes. I used jumbo rickrack for these flowers.

Rickrack Rosettes

1. Fold the rickrack in half and crisscross it back and forth over itself. You want it to stay flat, so try using a clipboard or binder clip to hold the fold, or put a pin through it to keep it from getting twisty.

2. Use a straight stitch on your sewing machine to sew down just one side of the crisscrossed rickrack, staying close to the edge. You can use the edge of the presser foot as a guide. Be sure to do a backstitch at the end of your stitching to keep things from unraveling.

Hint: The easiest way to make rickrack rosettes is with a sewing machine. But if you don't have one or don't know how to use one, you could hand stitch or hot glue the trim along 1 side instead.

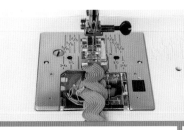

3. Begin making the rosette by coiling the cut end up a bit and adding a dab of hot glue. Then simply wrap the sewn trim around the coil, adding hot glue as you go to keep things in place.

4. At the end of the trim, simply tuck the trim under the bottom of the flower and hot glue it into place.

5. If you like, glue a little circle of felt to the underside of the flower to keep it sturdy and tidy looking.

You'll need 12˝ of ribbon to make a 2˝-wide ribbon flower. Use any width of ribbon you like (I used ⅜˝). Different widths will produce slightly different styles of flower. You will also need a needle and thread.

Loopy Ribbon Flowers

1. Thread your needle and tie a knot at the end of the thread (see Start with a Knot, page 16). Fold the ribbon over on itself by about 1˝ to make a loop. (If your ribbon has a design on one side, make sure the design stays on top and shows all the way around the loop.) Use your threaded needle to come up from the bottom of the loop, make one stitch, and bring it back under the loop.

2. Make another loop the same size as the first, and let the loose end of the ribbon go under the first loop. Push the needle down through the new loop and bring it up through all the layers of ribbons to sew another stitch.

3. Make a third loop between the first 2 and take another stitch through all the layers.

4. Make and stitch down 2 more loops to make a star shape with 5 loops.

5. Finish your flower by adding a few extra stitches and tying a knot underneath (see End with a Knot, page 17). You can add a center to the flower if you like, but these flowers are cute without it, too!

These flowers are kind of like the bow you would find on top of a present, only they don't have a center. That's the fun part! You can add a button, one of those pompom flowers you made earlier (page 21), a bunch of beads, or anything.

You'll need a ¾˝ felt circle, 6 pieces of ⅜˝-wide ribbon each 4½˝ long, a hot glue gun (page 125), and 3˝ of mini pompom trim to make a flower about 4˝ wide.

Daisy Ribbon Flowers

1. Form a loop with each piece of ribbon by hot gluing the ends on top of each other. Make 6 loops.

2. Hot glue the ends of each loop around the edges of your little felt circle.

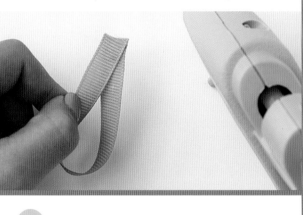

3. Finish your flower by gluing a tiny pompom flower (see Mini Pompom Flower Puffs, page 21) to the center of the other side of the flower.

Loopy little daisies are sweet on their own, but you can also layer the pieces to make bigger, fuller flowers if you like. Add a pin on the back and you have a darling brooch. Or glue a whole garden of these to a frame, your backpack, or maybe a mirror!

You'll need a 4˝ × 4˝ square of felt and a bit of hot glue (page 125) to make a flower about 2˝ wide.

Felt Wind-Up Flowers

1. Start off by rounding off the corners of your felt.

2. Choose any corner and start cutting just below it around the perimeter to make a ½˝-wide strip. Keep cutting around in a spiral until you get to the center of the felt.

3. Begin winding up the strip you have cut. Start coiling where you began cutting on the outside and just wind it right up. Add a dot of hot glue after each wind to help keep your flower together. You'll see a pretty flower starting to take shape!

4. When you're done winding, hot glue the little comma-shaped bit at the end to the bottom. Now you can start attaching Felt Wind-Up Flowers to anything you can think of!

These are so fun to make, you'll want to add them to everything!! I like to layer colors together. Sometimes I cut my strip with an uneven wavy edge to look more like petals.

You'll need a 10″ piece of 1″-wide felt, a bit of hot glue (page 125), and scissors to make a flower about 2″ wide.

Notched Felt Fluffs

1. Put a line of hot glue close to one edge of the felt strip. Fold the piece over to form a ½″-wide strip 10″ long. Press down firmly along the glued edge. If you prefer, you can fold the strip and sew the edge instead.

2. Use a pair of scissors to carefully cut ⅜″-long slits in the folded edge of the strip. *Don't cut from the glued edge!* Cut close to the glue, but make sure not to cut all the way through the strip!

3. Wind up your slit strip of felt and hot glue the end. Add a dot of hot glue after each wind to help keep the flower together. When your flower is wound up, cut a circle of felt to glue in place over the bottom. There you go! Another new talent!

Can you tell I love felt? I love it almost as much as I love flowers! Notched Felt Fluffs are great because they can be used on their own or combined with other embellishments to completely change their look. I especially like to glue pin findings to the back of these flowers and pin them to my coat, scarves, and purse!

I used 24˝ of ⅜˝-wide grosgrain ribbon and a hot glue gun (page 125). You can make these ferns with any sort of ribbon of any width. The wider the ribbon, the bigger your flower will be.

Ribbon Ferns

1. Begin by making a fold about 1˝ from the end of the ribbon. Dab a bit of hot glue under the end of the ribbon to hold the fold in place.

2. Make another fold, keeping the loopy part about the same size. Tilt this loop off to the side a bit. Hot glue it into place and then do another loop off to the other side. Hot glue that part into place and then make one more loop back to the middle of your flower. Hot glue it into place, but don't cut anything off.

I used this style of flower on the Glittery Name Frame (page 110), but it is sweet enough to attach to almost anything you dream of—what about a headband or a barrette? Just darling!

3. Once you've made the top of your flower, you can repeat Steps 1 and 2, making each row of loops just a smidge bigger than the last row and gluing them a little lower than the last row. This will create a flower that is tapered, which means it is a bit narrower at the top and nice and wide at the bottom. If you prefer a more feathery-looking bloom, make all your loops about the same length and add a few more layers. You might want to start with ribbon right off the spool and trim it when it's the size you want.

For each ribbon point, you'll need a 5˝-long piece of ⅝˝-wide ribbon and a hot glue gun (page 125).

Ribbon Points

1. Place a dot of hot glue in the center of a ribbon. Fold the ribbon in half in an L shape where it is glued.

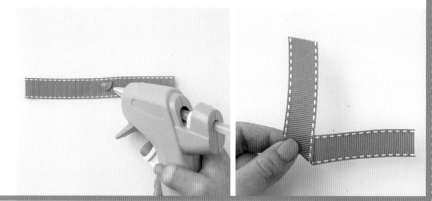

2. Put a dab of hot glue on top of the fold. Then, fold one end of the ribbon L back on itself at the fold. Trim the ends to make them even.

These little points don't look like much on their own, but they are quick and easy to make and can be used to make pretty shapes and patterns, like trees, leaves, feathers, or flowers. I used them to make the Holiday Hoop Ornament (page 106) and the Feathery Headband (page 64).

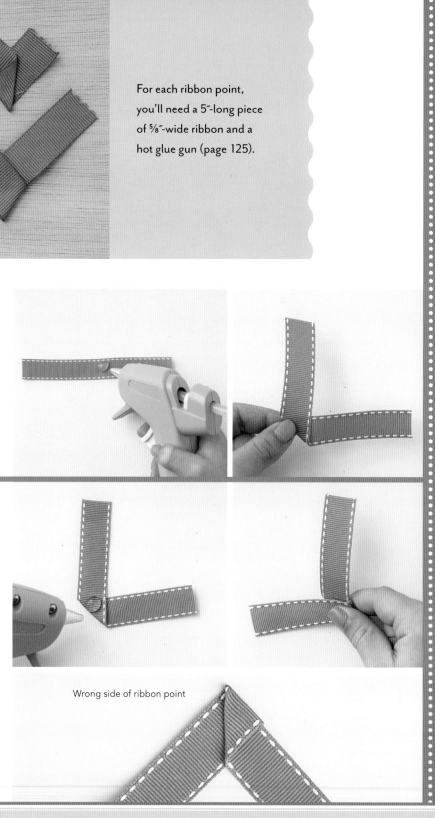

Wrong side of ribbon point

You'll need 8½˝ of ⅝˝-wide ribbon and a hot glue gun (page 125) to make a leaf that is about 2˝ tall.

Ribbon Leaves

1. Fold the piece of ribbon in half to find the center. Put a dab of hot glue in the fold, and then fold and press the ribbon together at the center to create a V.

2. Fold one end of the ribbon down to the bottom of the V, add a dab of hot glue, and press to glue it in place.

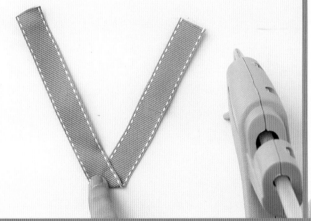

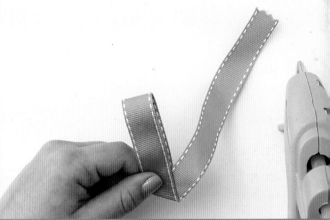

3. Fold the other end of the ribbon down to the bottom of the V on the opposite side. Glue it in place in the same way.

Ribbon leaves are handy for lots of different projects! You can even pile them together to make a flower.

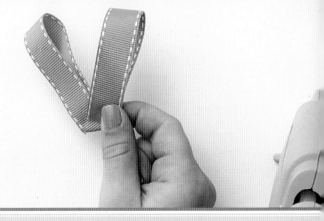

This makes a perfect bow every time. The secret is that there's no knot!

You'll need some ribbon—cut into 2 pieces 8½" long and 1 piece 2" long. You'll also need a hot glue gun (page 125). You can make this with any width ribbon you like—mine is ⅝" wide. You may want to cut longer lengths when using wide ribbon to make bigger bows.

Pretty Bows

1. For the loops at the top of the bow, put a dab of hot glue on the wrong side of each end of a long piece of ribbon. Fold the ends to the center, on the wrong side of the ribbon, and press down.

2. Squeeze the center where the ribbon ends meet together. Hot glue it at the back to hold it in place.

3. To make the tails of the bow, fold the other long piece of ribbon over on itself at an angle, and then fold it over again. The right side of the ribbon should be facing up on both tails. Put a dot of hot glue between the folds if you like.

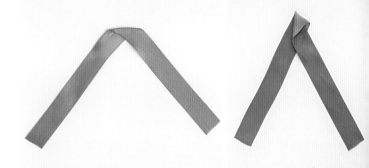

4. Glue the loop piece, right side up, on top of the tail, also right side up.

5. Wrap the short piece of ribbon around the center of your bow and hot glue it in the back. Trim any extra ribbon at the back.

This is my favorite bow. It's super easy, and there are lots of ways to change it up if you want to.

If you are attaching your bow to a blank (see *findings* in Good-to-Know Glossary, page 124), like a barrette or an elastic hair band, wrap the center ribbon around the front of the bow AND the piece you want to attach it to. Then hot glue the middle piece in place underneath.

Attach these lovely bits to anything and everything! Bows are the best—for adorning presents, hair accessories, or even T-shirts. Layer different ribbons on top of each other before making your bow to add lots of additional interest. Don't be afraid to experiment! Who knows what you'll come up with!

section 2

Happy
Hangout

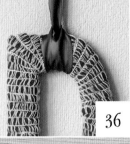

Initial Impressions **36**

Rickety Rack Room Pillow **51**

Mini Corkboard **39**

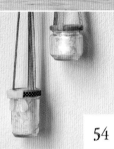

Sparkling Lantern **54**

Gleeful Garland **44**

Catchall Nests **58**

Sunny Lampshade Chandelier **48**

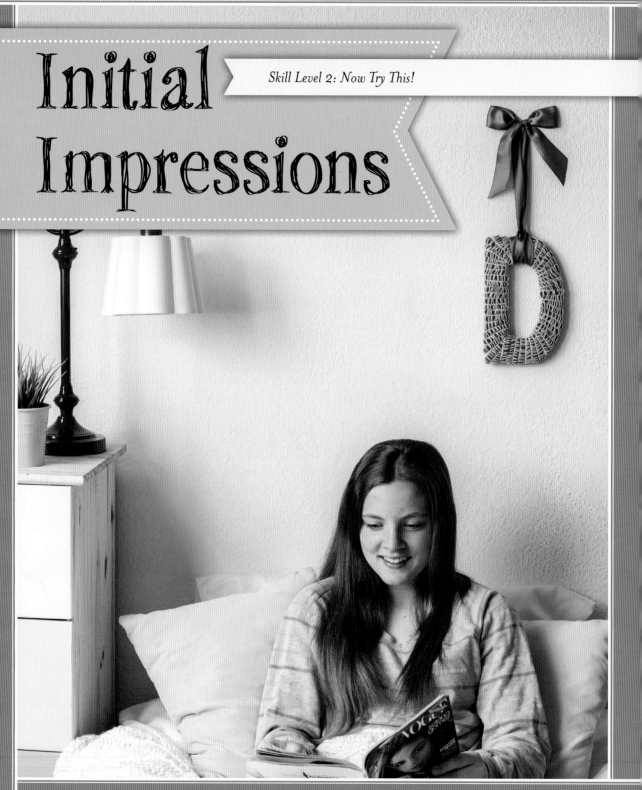

Initial Impressions

Skill Level 2: Now Try This!

A bit of glue, a bit of wrapping, and you'll have a lovely piece of art to brighten up your room and add a personal touch to your space. You can use a store-bought letter made of wood, or you can just make one yourself by drawing a letter on thick cardboard and cutting it out. ***There are lots of options to make this project uniquely yours, but let's make it EASY first.*** Then you can decide how you want to make it FABULOUS!

What You'll Need

Wooden letter, or thick cardboard to make your own

Yarn for wrapping

Hot glue gun (page 125)

Scissors

Ribbon for hanging

Hint: Choose a nice, thick yarn to wrap your letter. You could use thinner yarn, but that would take a LONG time to finish wrapping! A nice chunky yarn will help you get things all wrapped up in no time. Then you can get on to the "Making It Fabulous!" part at the end of the project. That part is always my favorite!

Make It Easy!

1. If you're using cardboard, draw a letter shape on the cardboard and cut it out.

Hint: If you slightly overlap the yarn as you wrap, it will be easier to cover the entire letter and keep any background colors from showing through.

2. To start wrapping your letter in its pretty yarn "sweater," just put a nice dab of hot glue on the back side of the letter at one corner and attach the yarn Pass the yarn around the letter and continue wrapping it around the letter.

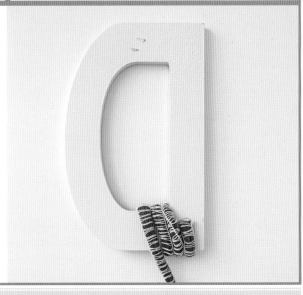

3. As you wrap, place an occasional dab of hot glue on the back of the letter to help hold the yarn in place. When the whole letter is covered, bring the yarn to the back again, snip it off, and hot glue the end into place.

4. Loop a ribbon at the top of your letter and tie the ends in a bow to hang! If your letter isn't easy to tie a ribbon around, you can glue or staple the hanging ribbon to the back.

Make It Fabulous!

Use ribbons, flowers, and felt embellishments to create an array of colorful flowers, buds, and leaves (see Here's How to Make It Fabulous!, page 18) and to add even more interest to your pretty letter. You could use this project to spell out your name, your initials, or a simple word like LOVE or HAPPY.

Mini Corkboard

This mini corkboard is the perfect size for hanging next to your bed or over your desk to help you remember important things. Or pin up pictures of your besties or your pet, instead of framing them.

What You'll Need

- Wood picture frame
- Grosgrain ribbon, ⅜˝ width
- Rickrack
- Felt (the size of your frame)
- Extra ribbon and trim for embellishing
- Sheet of cork, ¼˝ thick (as big as your frame)
- Piece of fabric a little larger than the sheet of cork
- Sand paper (if you're using a painted frame)
- Newspaper (optional to wrap the unused glass)
- Paint
- Paintbrush
- Ruler or tape measure
- Pen
- Ruler
- Scissors
- Hot glue gun (page 125)

Make It Easy!

1. Remove the back and glass from your frame. Set the back aside for now. If your frame is shiny, rub it gently with sandpaper before painting it.

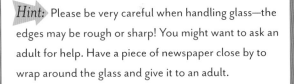

2. Make sure to protect your workspace from paint. Apply 2 coats of paint to the front of the frame. Let it dry completely after each coat.

Hint: Please be very careful when handling glass—the edges may be rough or sharp! You might want to ask an adult for help. Have a piece of newspaper close by to wrap around the glass and give it to an adult.

3. Trace the backing piece you took out of the frame in Step 1 onto your piece of cork. If you match the backing with one corner of the cork, you only have to trace 2 sides. Use sharp scissors to cut out the cork on the traced lines. Test it to make sure your cut cork fits in your frame. Trim it a little more if it's too big.

4. Lay the fabric out flat and place the cork on top.

Hint: If your fabric has a repeating pattern, make sure to center the design on the cork, so you don't cut off any pretty parts.

5. Cut the fabric, leaving an extra 1˝ border around the cork. Set the fabric aside for a moment!

6. Use a hot glue gun to place little dots of glue along the edge of the cork, one side at a time. Then center the fabric, right side up, over the cork. Press the fabric down onto the hot glue.

7. Flip the project over, so the fabric is facedown on the table and the cork is on top. Fold each corner of the fabric over the cork and hot glue it in place. Then fold each side of fabric over the cork and hot glue it in place.

Fold.   Fold.   Fold.

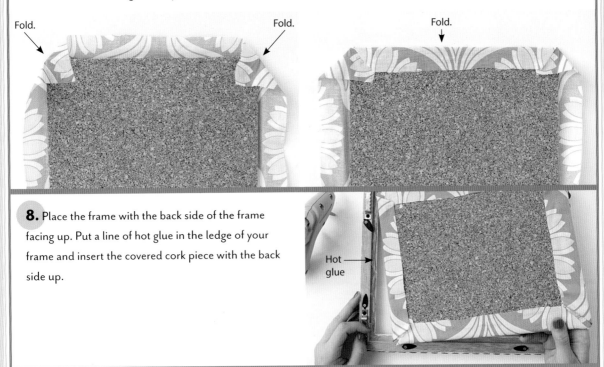

8. Place the frame with the back side of the frame facing up. Put a line of hot glue in the ledge of your frame and insert the covered cork piece with the back side up.

Hot glue

9. Measure the sides of the frame and cut the ribbons to fit. Fold under the ends of the ribbons and hot glue the pieces along the front and sides of the frame. You can use any ribbon you like! Choose just one or mix up the colors and styles.

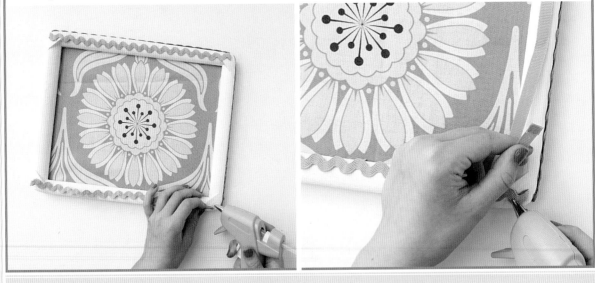

10. If you'd like to hang your project, fold a 9˝ piece of ribbon in half and hot glue it to the back.

11. Finish the project by cutting a piece of felt the size of your frame and hot gluing it over the back of the cork.

Make It Fabulous!

Embellish with felt flowers, buttons, satin rosettes, rickrack flower buds, or anything you like! I used Daisy Ribbon Flowers (page 25) and Notched Felt Fluffs (page 27).

Thanks for being such great friend! Love, Katie

Gleeful Garland

Skill Level 2: Now Try This!

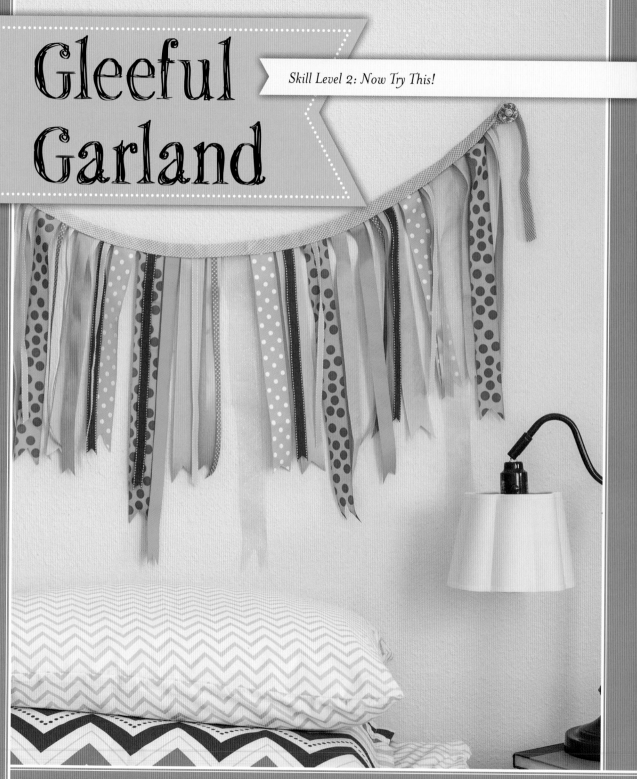

There's no quicker way to change the feel of a room than to add a festive garland! **This easy-peasy project is just the thing to add some interest to your windows, headboard, or that blank space over your desk.** You could even hang several sets of these from your ceiling!

What You'll Need

2 yards of ⅞″-wide bias tape (sold in the notions section of fabric stores)

15–25 yards of ribbon, or scraps 12″–20″ long (use various widths and types to add interest)

Scissors

Hot glue gun (page 125)

Pins

Hint: If you are making a garland for a smaller area—such as over your twin bed headboard—you might want to make it a bit shorter. Measure the space where you plan to hang your project and add one foot on each end, so you have enough seam binding to tie a pretty bow when attaching it to the wall.

Make It Easy!

1. Use a pin to mark the bias tape about 12″ in from each end. This will ensure you have enough space at the end to attach your garland wherever you'd like to hang it.

Hint: This project uses a mish-mosh of pretty ribbon scraps, but you could use ribbon in your school colors, fabric scraps, or crepe paper. You could even cut skinny strips from old T-shirts.

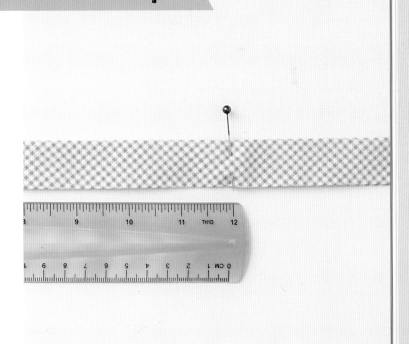

2. Start cutting *some* of the ribbons into pieces that vary from 12˜ to 20˜ long.

3. Before you finish cutting all the ribbons, lay out your ribbon pieces and decide on the arrangement of colors and widths that looks best. I used 46 pieces for this garland. Depending on the width of the ribbons you use, you may need more or fewer pieces.

Hint: Layer some of your thinner-width ribbons on top of wider ribbons to add even more interest!

4. Starting at the pin at one end, hot glue the ends of the ribbon pieces to the inside fold of the bias tape, and glue the bias tape down on top. Keep cutting and gluing ribbons in this manner, leaving about ¼˜ between each piece, until you reach the pin at the other end.

5. Fold the loose end of each ribbon piece with wrong sides facing. Cut at an angle toward the fold. This will take a little triangular notch out at each end of your ribbon pieces.

Oh, my goodness! Are you done already? Well, now that your garland is ready to hang, you can pop it up wherever you like. It would be cute over a window tied to a curtain rod, or try using removable adhesive hangers to drape it over your bed or desk! It's sure to make your room even more cheerful no matter where you put it.

If you are handy with a sewing machine, you could choose to sew your pieces in place rather than glue them—maybe use a zigzag stitch? So cute! Or embellish your garland with rickrack, beads, felt flowers, leaves, or other shapes. I used Rickrack Rosettes (page 23) and Felt Wind-Up Flowers (page 26).

Sunny
Lampshade Chandelier

Skill Level 3: You've Been Crafting Awhile!

Add more color and interest to your space with this fun project. It's a quick-and-easy way to update a light fixture or to create a pretty focal point for your room!

What You'll Need

Lampshade

⅜˝-wide grosgrain ribbon

⅜˝-wide satin ribbon

Pompom trim

Jumbo rickrack trim

Yarn

Hot glue gun (page 125)

Scissors

Hints

- Make sure your lampshade has metal pieces that connect the bottom ring to the top ring. Some lampshades don't, so when you cut away the fabric, you're left with two separate circles, and that won't do at all!

- Don't forget that the amount of trim you'll need will depend on the size of your shade and how you decide to trim it. If you choose a large lampshade, you'll need a good bit more ribbon or yarn. But if you choose an itty-bitty shade, you may need a lot less. A good rule is to double the height of the frame and use that amount for each vertical piece to be wrapped.

Make It Easy!

1. Cut away the fabric covering from the lampshade until you have just the metal frame.

2. Use either yarn or ribbon to wind around the frame, covering all the metal parts. I used yarn for the top and bottom and satin ribbon for the legs. Put a dab of hot glue on the frame to hold the ribbon or yarn; then wrap it around, overlapping just a bit. Glue down the end when a section is covered and cut off the loose end.

3. Cut a piece of jumbo rickrack the length of one leg of the frame. Glue the rickrack to the inside of a leg of the frame to create a scalloped look. Repeat this step for all the legs of the frame.

4. Measure the height of the frame from top to bottom. Add ½˝ to this number. Cut a piece of ⅜˝ grosgrain ribbon to this length for each midway point between the legs. Attach the ribbon midway between each leg by gluing the ends to the top and bottom of the frame.

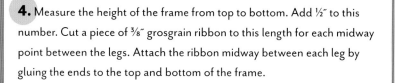

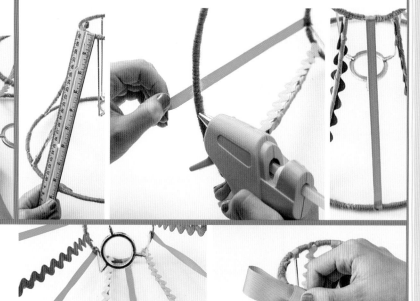

5. Glue pompom trim to the bottom circle of the frame. Tie 4 small bows or make 4 Pretty Bows (page 32) from ribbon. Glue a bow to the top of 4 legs of the frame. If there are more than 4 legs on your frame, space them evenly around the top.

Make It Fabulous!

Use your lampshade on a lamp or hang it from a piece of ribbon or cord over your bed or desk as a fun focal point for your room.

Add additional bows or rosettes for extra fun accents! What else could you add to your lampshade? Embroidered felt leaves, glittered cardboard stars, beads—the possibilities are endless!

Rickety Rack
Room Pillow

Aside from being soft and comfy, **a pretty pillow will look great in your room.** Make one for an accent, or make a whole pile to make things extra cozy!

What You'll Need

½ yard of fabric for the pillow, or 2 pieces at least 14˝ × 18˝ if you want to use 2 different fabrics, like I did

½ yard of lightweight fusible interfacing, at least 15˝ wide

Iron

Rickrack and grosgrain ribbons

Polyester stuffing

Hot glue gun (page 125)

Sewing machine

Pins

Scissors

Needle and thread

Make It Easy!

1. Cut 2 rectangles 14˝ × 18˝ from the fabric for the pillow front and back. Cut 1 rectangle 14˝ × 18˝ from the interfacing.

2. Press the fabric to get out any wrinkles. Then follow the instructions that came with the interfacing to fuse it to the wrong side of one of the fabric rectangles. Always ask an adult for permission before using an iron and be very careful whenever using something that gets hot.

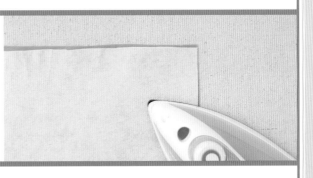

3. The fabric piece with the interfacing is the pillow front. Lay out rickrack and ribbon on the right side of the pillow front.

Layer the pieces over and under in a pattern you like and pin the pieces in place. Try layering narrower trim on top of wider trim. You can make your project like mine, or you can make it a design all your own!

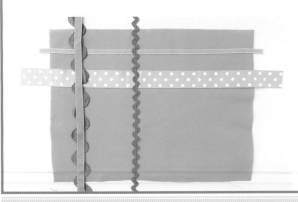

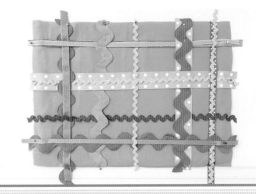

4. Starting on one side of your pillow, put a dot of hot glue under the ends of each ribbon to hold it in place. If you know how to use a sewing machine, you can straight or zigzag stitch your ribbons instead, but be sure to ask an adult first!

5. Trim off the excess ribbon so that it is even with the edges of the pillow front.

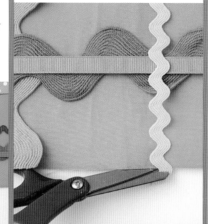

Hint: If you are layering ribbons on top of each other before you weave them, go ahead and glue them together before attaching them to your fabric pillow front. That way they won't slip slide away and make things tricky!

6. Place the front and back pieces of fabric with right sides together. Pin around the outside edges, leaving a 4˝ opening for stuffing! Put 2 pins on each side of the opening, so you won't stitch past this spot.

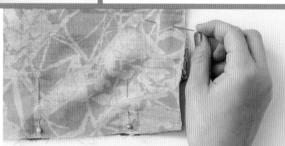

7. Starting at the double pin, sew all around the pillow, about ½˝ from the edge. Backstitch at the beginning and end of your seam.

8. Turn your pillow right side out through the opening. Use a pointed tool, like a chopstick, to poke the corners out from the inside. Iron the pillow cover on low heat and then stuff it nice and full of polyester stuffing!

9. When your pillow feels nice and firm, pin the opening and hand stitch it closed.

Now toss it on a chair in your room and enjoy your lovely new decor!

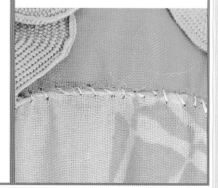

Sparkling
Lantern

LOVE ♥

Soft lighting will make your room a magical place! The next time you host a sleepover, **turn out the lights and turn on your sparkling lantern.** Everything will feel cozy and relaxing by faux candlelight!

What You'll Need

Clean jar (A new canning jar, a small glass jar from a craft store, or any old jar you rescued from the recycling bin will do—I like to use straight-sided jars.)

Fabric, felt, or scrapbook paper to cover the jar lid

Ribbon for around the lid

Paper doily or lacy craft paper (I used a clear plastic sheet with a lace pattern printed on it so light would shine through it.)

3 pieces of ribbon, each 11˝ long, to hang your lantern

1 piece of ribbon, at least 20˝ long, for a bow

Flameless tea candle (battery powered—very cool!)

Hot glue gun (page 125)

Scissors

Clear tape

Hint: If you don't have a paper doily or lacy craft paper, you can use a plain sheet of white paper. Just fold it like an accordion and cut shapes out of the folds to turn your paper into a snowflake. Then trim it to size. It will be perfect!

Make It Easy!

1. Turn the jar lid upside down and trace it onto a pretty piece of fabric, felt, or craft paper.

2. Cut out the shape and hot glue it to the top of the lid.

3. Cut a piece of ribbon to go around the rim of the lid and glue it in place.

4. Place the paper-covered lid right side down. Position the 3 long pieces of ribbon, right sides facing down, and hot glue them to the inside of the lid.

5. Turn the lid over, gather the 3 ribbons, and tie them into a knot.

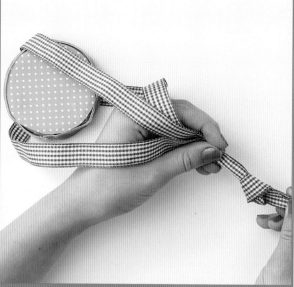

6. Make a Pretty Bow (page 32) and glue it over the knot.

7. Measure the height and length around your jar. Cut a rectangular piece of lacy craft paper that is ½˝ less than the height and the same length. So, if your jar is 4½˝ high and 6˝ around, cut your paper 4˝ × 6˝.

8. Roll up the paper and pop it into the jar. You may need to trim the paper a bit so that if fits right. If you do, just make tiny cuts! You can always trim off more, if necessary. Tape the ends of the piece of paper together inside the jar and pop your flameless candle inside.

9. Put the lid back on the jar. The ribbon might make it just a little tricky to get the jar closed, but you don't have to worry about it being super tight—just tight enough that bottom won't fall off! You can open it when you want to turn the candle on and off.

Your lantern is ready to hang!

Make It Fabulous!

Make a pretty felt rosette for the top of your jar, tie a lovely bow around the outside edge just under the lid, or add some other embellishment to the top of the hanging ribbons. Try making four or five lanterns from different sizes and shapes of jars, using all different kinds and colors of ribbons! A grouping like this would make a super fun focal point for an outdoor party, wouldn't it?

CAUTION!

You *must not* use a candle with a flame! This can cause the jar to get too hot to handle, burn the ribbon, possibly crack the glass, and potentially cause a fire! We do not want that to happen. So for your safety, please stick to the battery-powered flameless candle!

Catchall Nests

These darling little nest bowls will look sweet as pie on your desk holding paper clips, on your windowsill holding acorns, or on your dresser holding pretty hair clips. **They make a lovely present, too!** You could make one for your mom or granny or favorite teacher. It's such a fun project, you might want to make one for each of them!

What You'll Need

Waxed paper

Plastic wrap

Fabric stiffener (I like Aleene's Fabric Stiffener and Draping Liquid.)

Baker's twine (The amount you need depends on the size of your bowl, but plan on at least 10 yards.)

2 small bowls, 1 about 3˝–4˝ across the top of the bowl from side to side

Paintbrush

Paper towels

Make It Easy!

1. Cover your work surface with waxed paper. Wrap the outside of the 3˝ or 4˝ bowl in plastic wrap. Tuck any extra plastic wrap inside the bowl. Make sure the entire outside of the bowl is all the way covered. Then turn the bowl upside down on the waxed paper–covered surface.

2. Pour about ½ cup of stiffening liquid in the other bowl. Use your paintbrush to paint the very bottom (now the top) of your bowl with a nice thick layer of stiffener.

Hint: This is a pretty messy project! Plan to do this one in the kitchen, close to the sink. You'll need to rinse your hands pretty often!

3. Attach one end of your twine to the bowl by pressing it into the stiffener at the very center of your bowl. Start winding the twine on the top (bottom) of the bowl in a spiral.

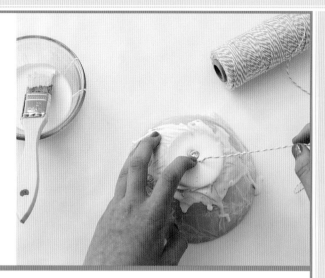

Hint: If the twine is sticking more to your hands than the bowl, take a break and wash and dry your hands. You'll also find it handy to keep a small bowl of water next to you while winding the twine around the bowl. If your fingers are a bit too sticky to push the twine into place, just dip them in the water and try again with a wet finger. Problem solved!

4. Cover the bottom of the bowl with twine. Then keep winding and layering it down the side of the bowl. Be sure to push the strands together as you go around. You can go around even MORE times to fill in any spaces that are not covered the first time. Bird nests are often a little messy and contain lots of layers!

Note

You can make your nest as deep as the bowl you are covering or you can make it shallower. If you make it shallower, it will look more like a nest. Do this by finishing the winding about halfway down the side of the bowl (or wherever you want!).

5. When you are done winding the sticky twine, use the paintbrush to thoroughly coat the baker's twine nest with a nice, thick layer of the stiffening liquid. It looks a lot like school glue, doesn't it?

Hint: Don't take the twine off the bowl while it's wet! Put your project somewhere that it won't be touched. Let it dry for at least 2 hours—letting it dry overnight works best.

6. When the outside feels very dry and stiff, turn the support bowl right side up and loosen the plastic wrap from the inside. Pull the stiffened twine off the support bowl and pull the plastic wrap off the bowl.

7. The inside of your nest bowl may still be a little sticky. Don't worry. Just put it in a nice dry place and give it a little while to finish drying. It will soon be ready to fill up with all your favorite bits!

section 3

Adornments

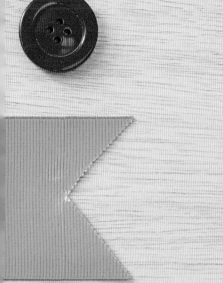

Feathery Headband

This is a quick-and-easy project and an absolutely **darling accessory that you'll wear all the time!** You could make this feather in your school colors to show a little extra spirit at your next pep rally.

What You'll Need

9 pieces 5˝ long of ⅝˝-wide ribbon (any type of flat ribbon)

Hot glue gun (page 125)

Scissors

Pinking shears

Flexible tape measure

1˝-wide elastic

Needle and thread

Sewing machine (*optional*)

Make It Easy!

1. Make 9 Ribbon Points (page 30). You can make them all from the same ribbon or mix up colors and patterns according to what you like.

2. If you have used more than one type of ribbon, decide how you would like to arrange the points. Lay them out from top to bottom, so they are pointing down like a V with the right side of the ribbon showing (the side without any extra folds).

3. Flip the ribbon points over so that you are working from the wrong sides. Take the *bottom* ribbon point, put a dot of hot glue on the tip of the V, and press the next ribbon point down on top of the bottom one.

4. Keep layering until you have glued all but one of the ribbon points together in a line.

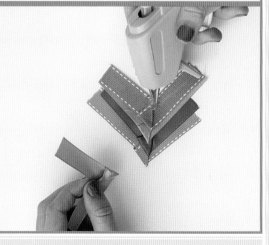

5. Glue the final point *upside down* at the very top.

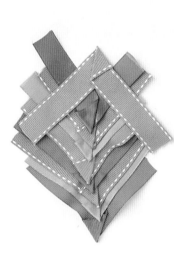

6. Don't worry if your feather looks a bit misshapen! Draw a feather or stretched oval shape on a piece of paper and cut it out. You can use this shape as a pattern to help trim your ribbon with the pinking shears and fix that right up!

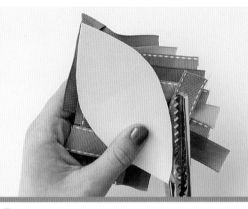

7. Use a flexible tape measure to measure around your head. Cut a piece of elastic to this length. Overlap the ends of the elastic so it fits snugly on your head. Sew the ends together with a sewing machine or hand needle and thread. Go back and forth a few times, or use the zigzag on your machine, or hand sew with big stitches.

8. Hot glue the feather, right side up, to the elastic right on top of the seam.

Make It Fabulous!

Add glue to the edges of your feather and dip it in glitter. Or try adding some simple embroidery stitches to give your piece extra color and texture.

Rocking

Skill Level 1: Start Here!

Pompom Ring and Earrings

You can customize this super quick-and-easy style of jewelry with your favorite colors. Find ring and earring blanks at your local craft or hobby store. Try a few variations using different-sized pompom trim and see what you can come up with!

What You'll Need

½ yard of mini pompom trim

Ring blank (page 125)

2 earring blanks (page 125)

Hot glue gun (page 125)

Scissors

Make It Easy!

1. Make Mini Pompom Flower Puffs (page 21). Use 11˝ of mini pompom trim for the ring and 3˝ for each earring.

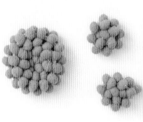

2. Hot glue your large flower to the ring blank and the mini flowers to the earring blanks.

Now you have the beginnings of a beautiful garden that you can take with you anywhere!

Make It Fabulous!

To make your ring even more fanciful, trace onto felt a flower or some other shape that is larger than your pompom flower. Cut it out and add a small slit in the center. Slide it over the ring blank from the back and glue it into place. You could also try this project with other ribbon flowers, like the Rickrack Rosette (page 23) or Satin Ribbon Rose (page 22)!

Layered Ribbon Belt

Skill Level 2: Now Try This!

The possibilities are endless! This simple belt can be as neutral or as crazy colorful as you like. Just choose a few different colors and widths of ribbon and see what you can come up with!

What You'll Need

1½˝-wide grosgrain ribbon (see Step 1 for length)

⅝˝-wide grosgrain ribbon (see Step 1 for length)

Sewing machine (*optional*)

Hot glue gun (page 125)

Flexible tape measure

Pins

2 D-rings

Make It Easy!

1. Measure your waist. Cut each piece of ribbon 11˝ longer than that measurement.

2. Lay the narrower ribbon on top of the wider ribbon and pin it in place. Use a straight stitch on a sewing machine to join the pieces by sewing down either side of the narrower ribbon.

Hint: If you don't have a sewing machine, you can use a hot glue gun to attach your layered ribbons to each other.

3. At one end of the layered-ribbon strip, fold the ends of the ribbon over ¼˝ and then fold another ¼˝ on the same end. Sew or hot glue the ends in place. This will tidy up any stringy edges and prevent fraying. This will be the loose end of your belt.

4. At other end of the ribbons, fold the end over ¼˝ to the wrong side and sew or hot glue it in place.

5. Place D-rings on top of each other and loop the end of the ribbon you just sewed through both rings. Stitch through all the layers of ribbon (or hot glue). Stay as close to the D-rings as you can, but leave enough room for them to wiggle just a bit.

6. Once the glue is dry, you can easily wear your belt by wrapping it around your waist, passing the ribbon through both of the D-rings and then passing it back through just one ring in the opposite direction. You can leave the tail of the belt hanging or tuck it around the side of the belt.

Make It Fabulous!

Make your belt even cuter by adding some fun stitching with your sewing machine! A zigzag stitch in contrasting thread colors will add another interesting element. Or add pretty buttons, a felt flower, or another layer of rickrack over your ribbon!

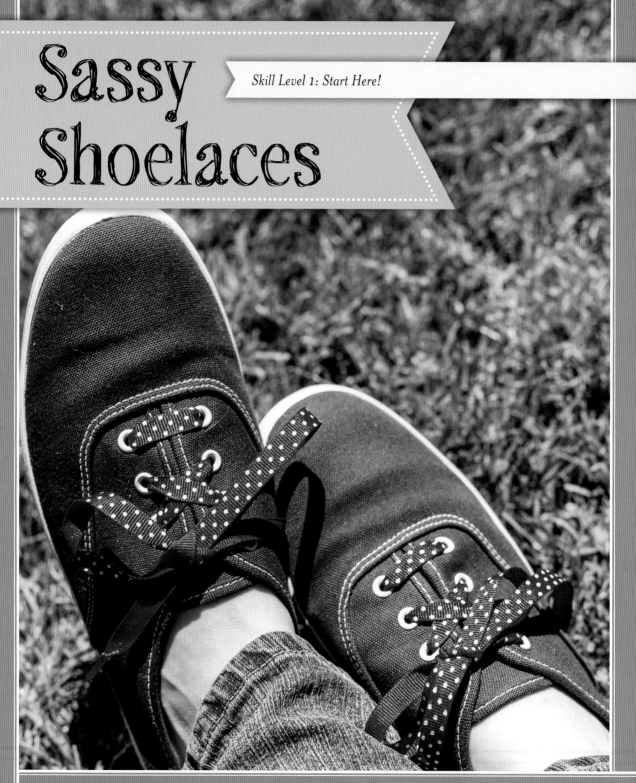

Sassy Shoelaces

Such fun! Switch out the laces in your old shoes for a *fun new fashion twist*. Or make a new pair of shoes a little more YOU by adding pretty ribbon laces with polka dots, stripes, or neon colors.

What You'll Need

⅜˝-wide ribbon (Measure 1 shoelace and double the length.)

Hot glue gun (page 125)

Hint: Grosgrain and woven ribbons make the best laces for shoes you wear and walk in a lot, because they don't fray as much as other types of ribbon. Satin ribbon makes a lovely bow, but the shiny, slippery fabric means your shoes will come untied—a lot! Save satin ribbon for shoes you don't wear that often.

Make It Easy!

1. Remove the shoelaces from your shoes and cut 2 pieces of ribbon the same length. Fold over each end of the ribbons about ¼˝ to the wrong side. Hot glue the folded end down.

2. Fold about ¾˝ at each end of the ribbon in half lengthwise. *Carefully* hot glue it closed. This makes narrow ends that are easy to thread through the eyelets of your shoes.

3. Pass your ribbon laces through the holes in your shoes.

Try using two different ribbons for a fun, contrasting look. You could use your school colors! Or try a soft, wide ribbon and tie a big, oversized bow at the top of your sneakers. So cute and way fun!

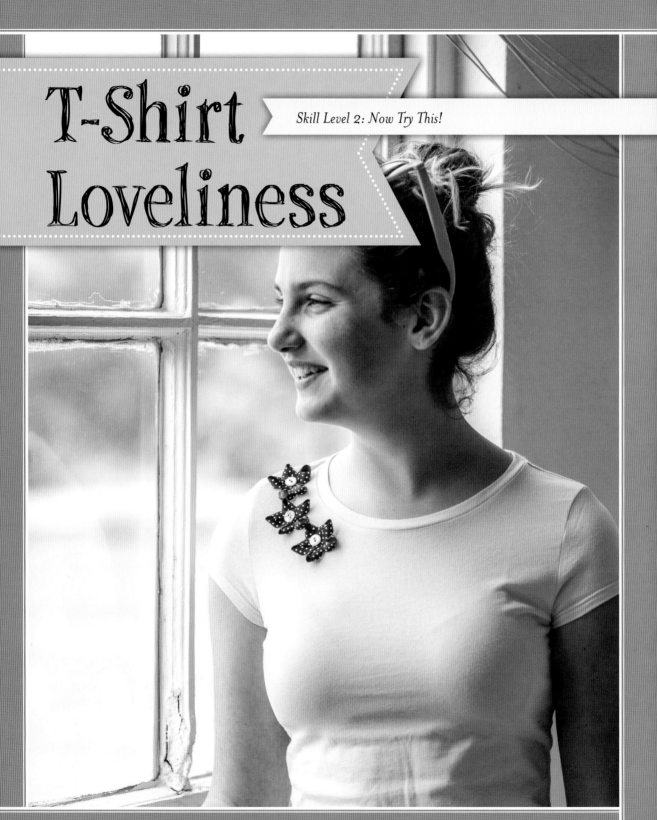

T-Shirt Loveliness

Adding just a bit of ribbon to a very simple T-shirt can make it into a one-of-a-kind top that is cute enough to wear to a party. I used the Loopy Ribbon Flowers (page 24) for this shirt, but you could use any of the ideas in Making Embellishments (page 18).

What You'll Need

1 yard ⅜″-wide ribbon (12″ for each of the 3 flowers)

T-shirt

3 small buttons

Needle

Embroidery floss

Scissors

Pins

Fabric glue (*optional*)

Make It Easy!

1. Make 3 Loopy Ribbon Flowers (page 24) to sprinkle on the shoulder of your favorite T-shirt.

2. Play around with the placement of the flowers on your T-shirt to decide where you like them. You can put them all close together to make a cluster on the shoulder, or you can sprinkle them closer to the bottom hem for a more casual look. Once you decide where you like them best, pin the flowers in place.

3. Use a needle and embroidery floss to sew buttons into the center of your flowers (see Sewing on a Button, page 14) and through the T-shirt. Start on the inside of the T-shirt and pass through the shirt, flower, and button a few times, ending on top of the shirt but under the flower. Tie a few knots (see End with a Knot, page 17) to keep the thread from coming loose.

Hint: If you want your flowers to stay nice and flat against your shirt, add a few dabs of fabric glue underneath each petal loop after sewing the flowers onto the T-shirt.

You'll want to wash your T-shirt by hand and hang it to dry.

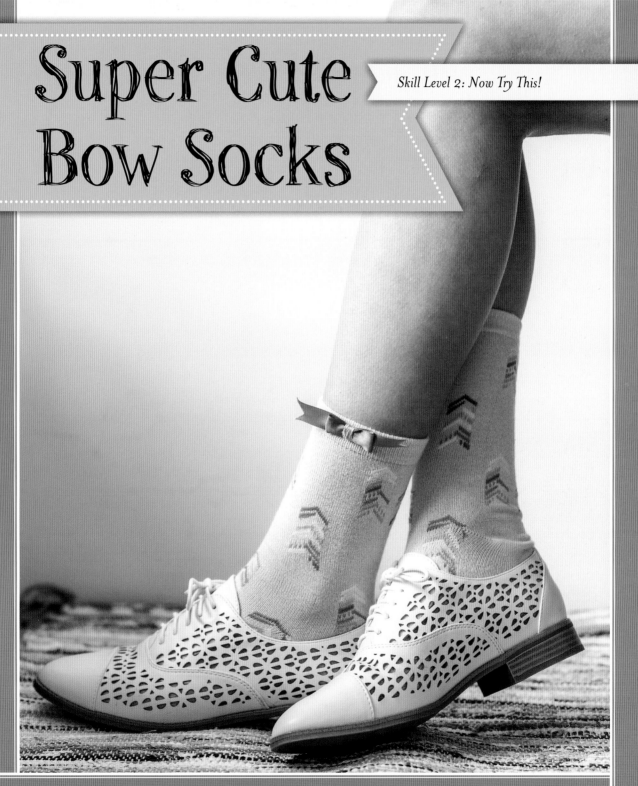

Super Cute Bow Socks

Socks are a fashion staple that never go out of style. We wear them with all sorts of outfits! I love cute socks with leggings or frilly socks with boots. **You can add even more unique style to your outfit by embellishing your socks with sweet little satin bows.**

What You'll Need

17˝ of ⅝˝-wide satin ribbon

Embroidery floss

Needle

Scissors

Pair of socks

Hot glue gun, *optional* (page 125)

Make It Easy!

1. Cut 2 pieces of ribbon 5˝ long for the top bow piece and 2 pieces 3½˝ long for the bottom bow piece.

2. Pinch one end of the 3½˝ long ribbon together and cut it at an angle toward the fold to make the pointy ends of the bow. Repeat this step for all 4 ends of the 3½˝ pieces.

3. Thread a needle with embroidery floss. Tie a knot in one end of the floss (see Start with a Knot, page 16). Push the needle from the inside of the sock to the right side of the sock at the top where you want the center of the bow to be. Set the sock aside for now.

4. Fold the ends of a 5˝ piece of ribbon to the middle, overlapping them slightly. If you want, add a dot of hot glue to hold it together in the center.

5. Place this folded piece on top of a bottom bow piece, folded-side down, on the sock where the thread is coming out.

6. Wrap the thread around all the layers at the center of the bow. Bring the needle to the bottom of the bow and sew back through to the inside of the sock.

7. Come up again through the sock at the top of the bow.

8. Repeat Steps 6 and 7 about 10 times, looping around your bow to the inside of the sock to form a pretty little centerpiece.

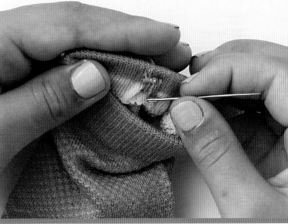

9. Finish by tying a knot (see End with a Knot, page 17) underneath the bow, inside the sock. Then trim the thread.

10. Repeat Steps 3–9 to add a bow to the other sock.

section 4

School

Spirit

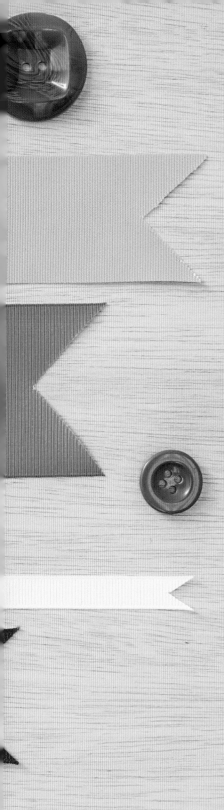

Fluffy Ribbon
Keychain

82

Ribbon-Edged
Paper Clips

95

Woven Notebook
Cover

85

Team Spirit Bow
Bobbies

98

Go Team!
Pennant Banner

89

Spirit Hair Bow

100

Spirit Pen or Pencil

93

Fluffy Ribbon Keychain

This project is super cute—and super useful. Sure, you can put your house key on the loop and never lose it again. But **you could also make this tassel in your school colors** and attach it to your backpack or gym bag, so you can show off your school spirit!

Satin and grosgrain ribbon: 9–12 yards total of at least 3 different ribbons (I used 6 different ribbons, so I didn't need as much of each.)

1 yard of ⅛"-wide satin ribbon

3" of ⅝"-wide satin ribbon

Key ring

Scissors

5" × 6" piece of cardboard

Tape

Hot glue gun (page 125)

Make It Easy!

If you wrap the shorter side of the cardboard, you'll get a shorter, fluffier keychain; if you wrap around the long side of the cardboard, your keychain will be a little longer.

1. Cut the skinny ⅛"-wide ribbon into 2 pieces, each about 18" long. Cut the rest of the ribbons into pieces either 40" (for a short, fluffy keychain) or 48" (for a longer keychain).

2. Gather the ends of all your long ribbon pieces in one hand. Tape the ends to one side of your cardboard.

3. Wrap the ribbons around the cardboard until they're all wrapped up.

4. Lay the cardboard on a table, with the loose ends of the ribbon facing down. Pass the piece of ⅛"-wide ribbon under all the layers and tie a knot at the top. Slip it on the key ring and tie another tight knot around it.

5. Cut through all the layers of ribbon along the bottom edge of the cardboard to turn the loops into a tassel. Set the cardboard aside.

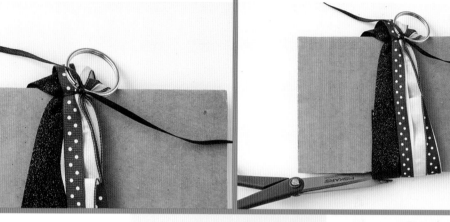

6. Gather all the ribbons tightly at the top, close to the key ring. Wrap another piece of ⅛" ribbon around the top of the loop, about 1" below the key ring, nice and snug. Tie a knot.

7. Hot glue a piece of ⅝" ribbon over the skinny ribbon knot to cover it and finish off your project.

8. Trim the ends of ribbon at the bottom of the tassel so they are even, if you need to.

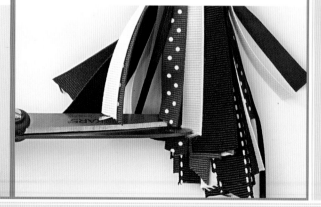

Woven Notebook Cover

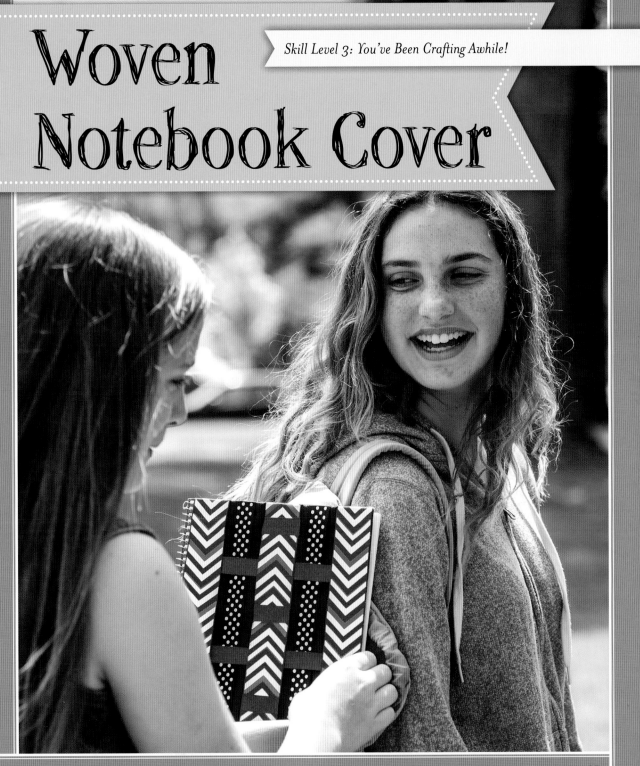

School can't happen without note-books, right? Sometimes it gets tricky to carry them all around, and sometimes it's hard to tell which one is for which class. But if you take a few minutes and a few spools of ribbon, **you can easily make your plain old notebooks into something super colorful** and fun!

What You'll Need

Spiral notebook

Ruler

Pen

Grosgrain and satin ribbons in various widths, including at least ⅔ yard of 1½˝-wide ribbon

Hot glue gun (page 125)

Felt, the same size as the notebook cover

Scissors

Make It Easy!

1. Measure the front cover of your notebook from top to bottom and add 1˝ to this measurement. Cut 2 pieces of the 1½˝-wide ribbon to this length. These will be the 2 outside warp pieces. Then cut enough pieces at this length from the other ribbons to cover the rest of the front of your notebook. These are the inner warp pieces.

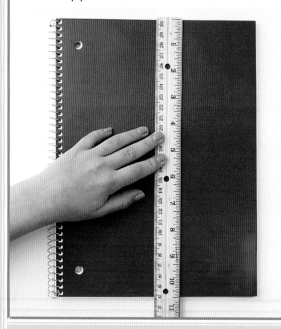

Hint: When weaving, *warp* refers to pieces that run from top to bottom of your project; *weft* refers to pieces that run from side to side.

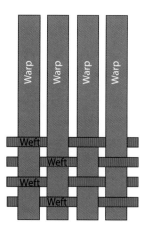

2. Measure the front cover of your notebook from side to side, subtract 1˝ from this measurement and cut enough ribbon pieces (weft) to cover the entire front of the notebook.

3. Arrange the warp strips in a pattern you like on top of your notebook.

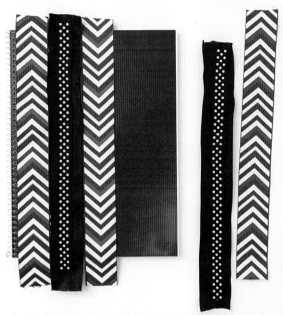

4. If you are layering any sets of warp strips, glue these together first, and then set them back in place on your notebook cover.

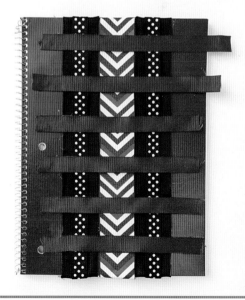

5. Pull off the warp strips on the outside left and right; you'll glue those in place later. Fold the ends of the rest of the warp strips over to the wrong side of the cover, and hot glue them in place. Check that they are staying straight before gluing the top and the bottom.

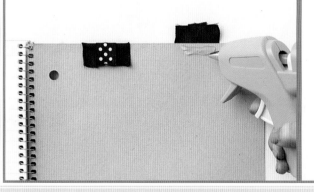

6. Arrange the weft strips on top of the warp pattern, but *don't* glue them yet.

7. Weave the weft strips in and out of the warp strips by passing them over and under each warp strip.

8. Place a dab of hot glue under the end of each weft piece of ribbon, all the way around your notebook.

9. Hot glue the left and right ribbons from Step 5 over the edges of your weft ribbons. Fold the ends over to the inside cover and hot glue them down.

10. Trim the piece of felt ¼″ smaller than your notebook cover and hot glue it to the inside cover to hide all the ribbon edges.

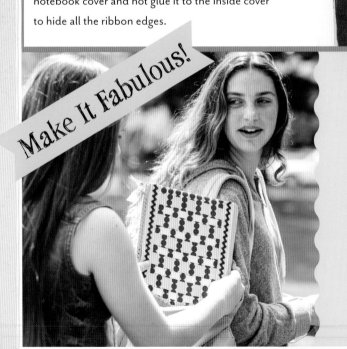

Make It Fabulous!

Make your notebook even more amazing by adding a ribbon pompom, a fancy two-tone bow, or an extra pocket inside! Or add all of these and create a super-special creation that you'll want to hold on to way after school is out for the summer!

Go Team! Pennant Banner

You don't have to be a cheerleader to support your team with lots of spirit! Try making this fun pennant banner for your next big team event. **You'll stand out from the crowd** with this sparkly creation that shows off your school spirit—big time!

What You'll Need

- 7½˝ × 17½˝ piece of canvas fabric
- Pencil
- Ruler
- Waxed paper
- Stiffening liquid (My favorite is Aleene's because it is so easy to clean up!)
- Plastic container or bowl
- Paintbrush
- Plastic wrap
- Paint, in your school or team colors
- Letter stencils, letter stickers, or wooden letters
- 24˝ of ½˝-diameter dowel
- Rickrack
- Hot glue gun (page 125)
- Grosgrain or satin ribbons in school or team colors
- Scissors

Make It Easy!

1. Fold a short side of the canvas rectangle in half to find the center. Make a mark at the fold with a pencil.

Fold in half.

2. Lay your ruler from the mark to the top corner of the other short side and draw a line.

3. Lay your ruler from the mark to the bottom corner of the other short side and draw a line.

4. Cut out the triangle-shaped pennant on the marked lines.

Cut on lines.

5. Cover your work surface with something waterproof to protect your table. Lay out a sheet of waxed paper and then put the pennant on top of the waxed paper.

6. Pour about 1 cup of stiffening liquid into a bowl and use the paintbrush to coat one side of the entire pennant several times.

7. Allow the stiffener to dry until only tacky. The pennant does not have to be completely dry. Turn it over on your waxed paper and coat the other side with stiffening liquid. Once both sides are coated, allow the pennant to dry completely.

Hint: While you are waiting for the first side to dry a bit, cover your stiffening liquid with a bit of plastic wrap to keep it from drying out.

8. Time to paint! Once again, protect your work surface. Using colors for your favorite team, paint the pennant. Allow it to dry before turning it over to paint the other side.

9. Use another color from your school or team to paint your dowel. Paint as much as you can with it lying flat. Let it dry and then turn it to paint the rest.

10. Hot glue some rickrack around the edges of one side of the pennant.

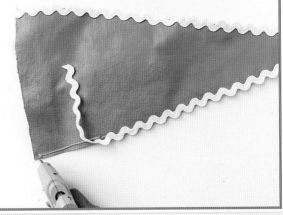

11. On the front of your pennant with the rickrack, glue down the letters or place stickers or stencils to add your team's name. Or you could add a phrase like "Win!" or "Go Team!"

12. Wrap the wide end of the pennant around the dowel and glue in place.

Make It Fabulous!

Use school glue to trace around your lettering. Dust the glue with glitter to give your banner lots of sparkle. Or poke more holes along the dowel rod through the banner and tie several strands of different-colored ribbons through each hole and around the dowel rod to create streamers that will blow around when you wave your banner!

13. Use scissors to make a small hole at the top of the pennant. Tie several ribbons through the hole and around the rod.

Spirit Pen or Pencil

There are many ways to show your school spirit, but this is one of the easiest! A bit of ribbon and glue will turn your favorite pen into a pretty way to show what team you support.

What You'll Need

Pen or pencil

25˝ of ⅜˝-wide grosgrain ribbon (Most pens and pencils are about 6˝ long. If yours is a different size, you may need more or less ribbon. You can leave the ribbon uncut until the project is finished.)

At least 17˝ of ⅝˝-wide ribbon (cut into 2 pieces 8½˝ long)

Hot glue gun (page 125)

Scissors

Make It Easy!

1. Put a dab of hot glue at the top of your pen or pencil. Press the ribbon into the hot glue and give it a second to set. Then rotate the pen to start wrapping it in ribbon.

2. As you wrap the ribbon around, be sure to overlap it just a little bit and add a dot of glue with every few wraps. Carry on all the way to the tip. Use another spot of glue to hold the end of the ribbon in place.

3. Repeat Steps 1 and 2 to wrap the cap of the pen, if there is one.

4. Make a Pretty Bow (page 32) from the ⅝˝ ribbon. Hot glue the bow to the top of your pen or pencil or to the pen cap.

Make It Fabulous!

Add an embellishment from Here's How to Make It Fabulous! (page 18) to the top of your pen if you want to make it even more unique!

Ribbon-Edged Paper Clips

This super-easy project will add lots of fun to your desk and school supplies. **You can use these little clips as bookmarks** or to keep a stack of papers tidy. A little batch of them in your school colors would make a cute present for a friend!

What You'll Need

Scraps of ribbon

Paper clips

Hot glue gun, *optional* (page 125)

Make It Easy!

All you need to do is cut all of your ribbon scraps to one length (I like 5˝). Then tie them on, one by one, to the end of your paper clip. Once they are tied on, tie a few of the wisps to each other. Super easy and totally fun, right?

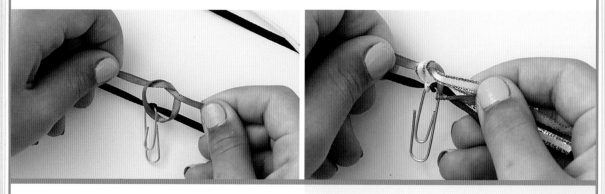

Hint: The smaller your paper clip, the narrower the width of ribbon you'll want to use. Or if you have a wider ribbon that you just love, use only one piece of ribbon. More isn't always better, right?

Here's another option for your clips: Cut a 3˝ piece of ⅜˝ ribbon, fold it through the clip, and glue the ribbon together.

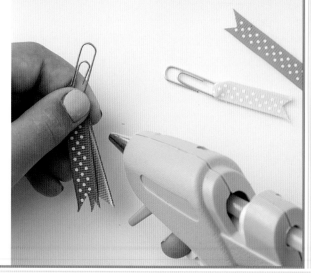

Make a whole slew of these to share! You can also use them to color code your schoolwork to make it easier to find things when you need them. Organization can be fun!

Team Spirit Bow Bobbies

Skill Level 1: Start Here!

Make these pretty accessories as an easy-peasy way to show your team spirit!

What You'll Need

5˝ of ⅞˝-wide grosgrain ribbon in your team colors

1½˝ of ⅜˝-wide grosgrain ribbon in your team colors

Bobby pins with pads

Hot glue gun (page 125)

Make It Easy!

1. Follow Steps 1 and 2 of Pretty Bows (page 32) to make 1 bow without tails. Use the ⅞˝-wide ribbon.

2. Follow Step 5 of Pretty Bows (page 33) to wrap the ⅜˝-wide ribbon around the center. Hot glue it on the back of the bow.

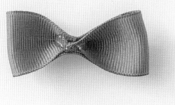

3. All that's left is attaching your sweet bow to a bobby pin. Dab some hot glue on the pad of the bobby pin and stick the little bow to it. Let it dry. Then tuck it in your hair. Simple as pie!

Wear your pretty bows to your next team event and everyone will wonder where you got your spirit wear. They'll never guess you made it yourself!

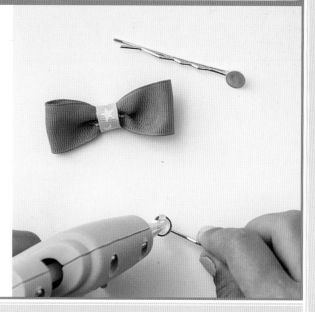

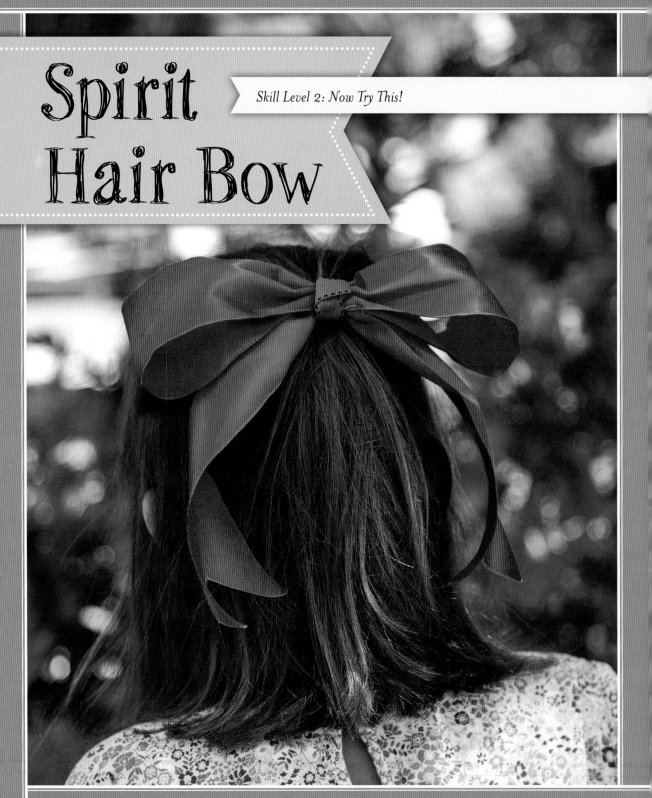

Spirit
Hair Bow

Skill Level 2: Now Try This!

Celebrate your team spirit by wearing this fun hair bow. ***It is a happy addition to any wardrobe*** and will go especially well with your school-day outfit if you make it in your team's colors! You may like this bow as a ponytail wrap, or you could attach it to a barrette. There are lots of options for this project—and they're all fun!

What You'll Need

2½˝-wide grosgrain ribbon

½˝-wide grosgrain ribbon

3˝ piece of wire or twist tie (like from a bread bag)

Hot glue gun (page 125)

Scissors

Elastic hair band or barrette clip

Make It Easy!

1. Cut 1 piece of 2½˝-wide ribbon 18˝ long for the loops and 1 piece 15˝ long for the tails.

2. Fold the longer piece in half and make a little crease. Open the longer piece of ribbon back up, fold the ends in to the center crease, and glue them in place.

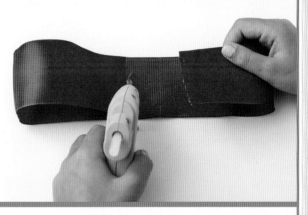

3. Squeeze the center of the loop together and hot glue it. These are the loops for the top of the bow!

4. To make the bow tails, pinch one end of the shorter ribbon together and cut it at an angle toward the fold to make the bow's pointy ends. Do the same thing on the other end of the piece.

5. Fold the tail ribbon piece in half by folding it over at the middle. Lay it down flat, so it looks like an upside down V.

6. Put the glued ribbon loop on top of the folded tails. Wrap the twist tie around both the loop and the tails at the center and twist tightly, gathering both sections of ribbon in the middle.

7. Snip off any extra bit of twist tie with sturdy craft scissors, or just twist it all around the center of the bow.

8. Cut a 3˝-long piece of the ½˝-wide ribbon. Tie a knot in the center, but don't pull it tight; leave it kind of open. Then press it down flat. This will make the center of your bow.

9. Hot glue the center knot over the front center of your bow. This piece will cover the twist tie and is used to attach the bow to your elastic band or barrette.

10. Turn over the bow and hot glue the elastic band or barrette to the back of bow. Fold the center ribbon over the band or barrette and hot glue it into place. Trim off any extra.

Make It Fabulous!

Attach these lovely bits to anything and everything! Bows are the best—for presents, hair accessories, and adorning T-shirts. Layer different ribbons on top of each other before making your bow to add lots of additional interest. Don't be afraid to experiment! Who knows what you'll come up with!

For a larger bow, use 3˝-wide ribbon.

If you want to add more color or variety to your hair bow, cut 2 pieces of 18˝ ribbon, but make sure one is wider than the other. Glue the narrower ribbon to the center of the wider ribbon and then form the bow following all the same directions. This is an easy way to add more color and team spirit to your project!

Pretty Handmade Presents

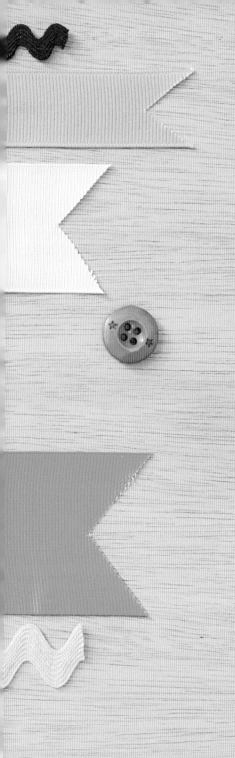

106

Holiday Hoop
Ornament

115

Stem and Leaf Tote

110

Glittery Name
Frame

118

Happy Day Cards

113

Rickrack Rosette
Bracelet

121

Let's Wrap It Up

Holiday Hoop Ornament

Skill Level 2: Now Try This!

This cute sparkly snowflake ornament *can easily be changed for any holiday* and makes a darling present for someone you love.

What You'll Need

Small embroidery hoop (Mine is 5˝ in diameter.)

1 piece of fabric at least 1˝ bigger all around than your hoop.

1¼ yards ⅝˝-wide grosgrain or satin ribbon

1¼ yards sequin string (These are pre-threaded onto a cord, not the loose kind.)

Sparkly button or large bead, about 1˝ in diameter

12˝ of ¼˝-wide satin ribbon for hanging loop

20˝ of ⅜˝-wide satin ribbon for bow

1 piece of felt at least 2˝ bigger all around than your hoop

Scissors

School glue, Fray Check, or clear nail polish (*optional*)

Hot glue gun (page 125)

Make It Easy!

1. Open the embroidery hoop and insert the fabric. Close the hoop and trim the excess fabric from the back.

2. From both the ⅝˝-wide ribbon and the sequin string, cut 4 pieces 5˝ long and 4 pieces 4˝ long.

3. Glue the cut sequin strings down the center of the same-size ribbon pieces. Make sure to add hot glue, school glue, Fray Check, or clear nail polish to the loose ends of the sequin strings to keep them from unraveling. Then fold the doubled pieces and join the ends with a bit of hot glue to form a loop.

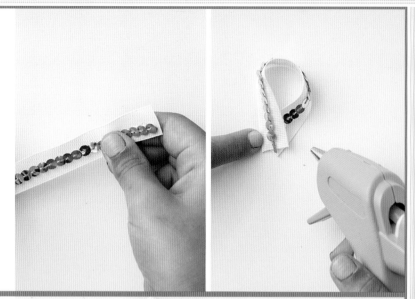

4. With the 4 bigger loops, press the top of each loop flat with your finger, so that it forms a pointy tip. On the wrong side, add a dab of hot glue in each corner of the tip.

5. Arrange the bigger loops on the hoop in the shape of an X. Then arrange the smaller loops in a plus sign to make your snowflake. Hot glue all of the pieces in place.

Hint: Be sure that the screw top of the hoop is situated directly above the snowflake when you are gluing the pieces to the fabric.

6. Trace the hoop onto the felt and cut it out. Hot glue the felt circle to the back of the hoop.

7. From a scrap of the felt, cut out a circle just a bit larger than the button or bead. Glue the button or bead onto the little felt circle and then hot glue it to the center of the snowflake.

8. At the top of your hoop, use the ⅜˝ satin ribbon to tie a bow around the hoop's screw top. Then use the ¼˝ ribbon to tie a knot around the screw. Knot the ends to make a loop for hanging.

Make It Fabulous!

Try this ornament using the Ribbon Points technique (page 30). Or switch up your project for different holidays or occasions!

Glittery Name Frame

What You'll Need

- Wood picture frame
- Sandpaper (if you're using a painted frame)
- Craft paint
- Paintbrush
- Wood letters
- White school glue
- Glitter
- 1½–2 yards ⅜″-wide grosgrain ribbon (depending on the size of your frame)
- Hot glue gun (page 125)
- Scrapbook paper at least the size of your frame
- Newspaper (*optional*)
- Baker's twine for the flower stem

Make It Easy!

1. Remove the backing and glass from your frame. If your frame is already painted or is very shiny, sand it lightly with sandpaper.

Hint: Please be very careful handling glass—the edges may be rough or sharp! You might want to ask an adult for help. Have a piece of newspaper close by to wrap the glass and give it to an adult.

2. Cover your work surface to protect it. Paint the front and sides of your frame with craft paint and let it dry. Apply a second coat of craft paint and let it dry.

3. Apply 2 coats of paint to the front and sides of the wood letters and let them dry after each coat. When they are dry, spread white school glue over the front of the letters and dust with glitter.

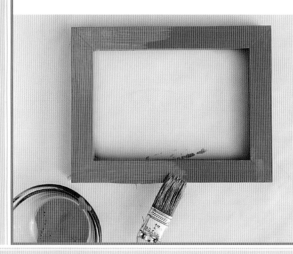

4. Decide which way you want your frame to sit. Cut 2 pieces of ribbon, each 1″ longer than the width of your backing.

5. Flip the frame so the back side is up. Hot glue the ribbon pieces across the middle of the frame, inside the ledge that the backing will sit in. Cut off any extra ribbon that sticks out of the back.

6. Trace the cardboard backing from your frame onto the scrapbook paper and cut it out.

7. Glue the paper to the cardboard with white school glue. Let it dry. Put hot glue around the edges of the frame opening and press the covered backing in place.

8. Arrange the letters at the top of the frame to spell out the name you want. Hot glue the letters to the frame.

9. Make a Ribbon Fern (page 28). Cut a piece of ribbon or braid some baker's twine for a stem. Glue the stem, then the embellishment, to the side of the frame.

Make It Fabulous!

You have made a lovely present. If you are still feeling crafty, add a few more details to "Make It Fabulous!" What about a button border? Or glitter around the outside edges? Remember to let your creativity shine through!

Rickrack Rosette Bracelet

I am very partial to flowers. Can you tell? I love this bracelet, not just because it has lovely, little Rickrack Rosettes (page 23), but also because **it is super quick and easy to make and is a really cute present!** Find bracelet blanks at your local craft or hobby store.

What You'll Need

3 yards rickrack

Hot glue gun (page 125)

Bracelet blank (page 125)

Hint: If you want to make each flower a different color, you will need at least 20˝ of rickrack for each flower.

Make It Easy!

1. Make 5 Rickrack Rosettes (page 23).

2. Guess what? You're almost done! All you need to do is glue those sweet little rosettes to your bracelet blank and ta-da! You are finished. You have a lovely, new, handmade accessory. Or the perfect gift for your favorite friend!

Stem and Leaf Tote

Skill Level 2: Now Try This!

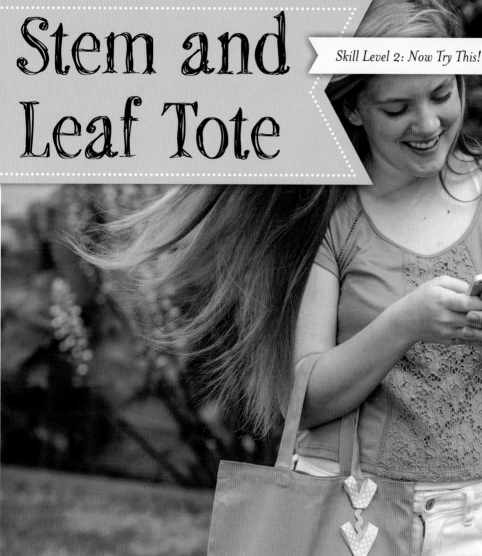

Not too big and not too small, **this tote is just right for your gym clothes, dance wear, or a trip to the library.** There are lots of ready-made totes to choose from at your local craft store, and they come in many pretty colors!

What You'll Need

Canvas tote

1 yard of ⅝˝-wide ribbon

1 piece of rickrack (as long as your tote bag is high)

Sewing machine or hot glue gun (page 125)

Pins

Make It Easy!

1. Cut the ribbon into the following 5 lengths: 8½˝, 7½˝, 6½˝, 5½˝, and 4½˝.

2. Make a Ribbon Leaf (page 31) from each length of ribbon.

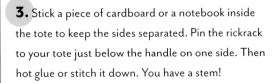

3. Stick a piece of cardboard or a notebook inside the tote to keep the sides separated. Pin the rickrack to your tote just below the handle on one side. Then hot glue or stitch it down. You have a stem!

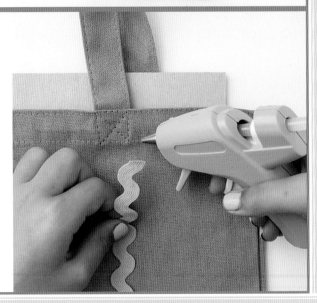

4. Place the leaves on the stem, with the biggest leaf lowest down. You can space them far apart or mush them all up close—whatever you prefer. Once you've decided, pin and then hot glue or stitch them in place.

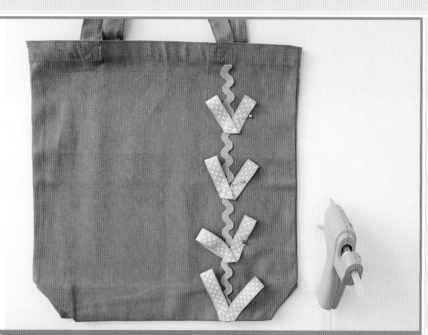

Make It Fabulous!

That didn't take long, did it? Are you still in a crafty mood? Add a Felt Wind-Up Flower (page 26) to the top of your stem. Or apply a few embroidery stitches over your stem. If you can use a sewing machine, try adding a few rows of stitches in a coordinating color around the top of your tote. Sweet and simple!

Happy Day Cards

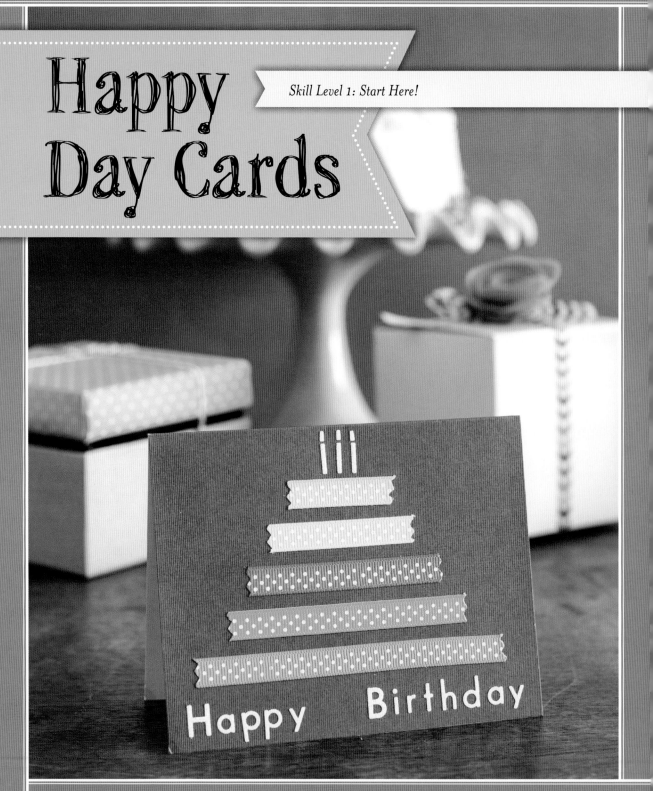

A handmade card is a sweet way to let someone know you care. This quick project is nice for a birthday greeting. Or use your imagination to make this project into a holiday card!

What You'll Need

At least 20˝ of ⅜˝-wide ribbon
(I used scraps of 5 different colors.)

Blank 4¼˝ × 5½˝ premade card or 8½˝ × 11˝ piece of cardstock to make your own

Hot glue gun (page 125)

Scissors or decorative-edge scissors

Markers or stick-on letters

Make It Easy!

1. If you are making your own card, fold the cardstock in half through the longer side.

2. Cut the ribbon in the 5 following lengths: 5˝, 4½˝, 3˝, 3½˝, and 2˝. I used my pinking shears to get a zigzag edge to my cut.

3. Lay the ribbon on the front of the card from longest to shortest piece. Hot glue each to the card. Leave some space at the bottom to add your phrase.

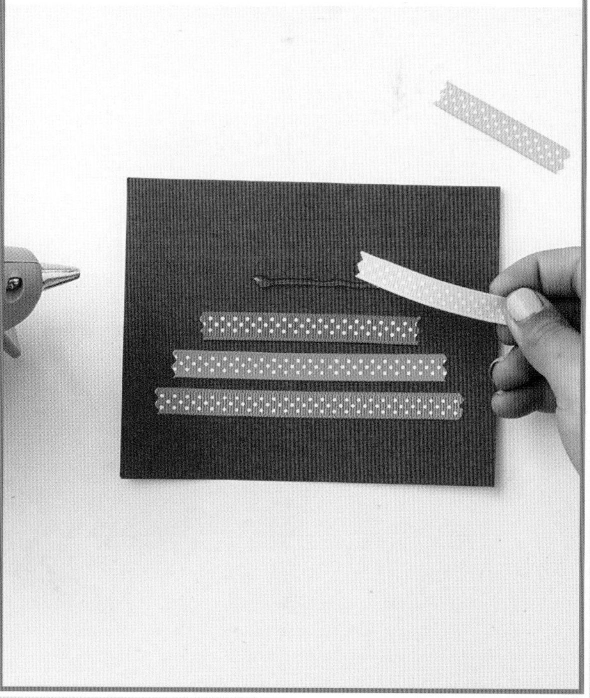

4. Add the lettering. I used stickers, but you could also write something.

Make It Fabulous!

Use school glue to add pattern and detail to your card. Then, while the glue is still wet, carefully pour glitter over the glue. Shake off any excess after the glue dries. Use trims, paint, markers, or stickers to add even more detail if you like!

Happy ♥ Birthday

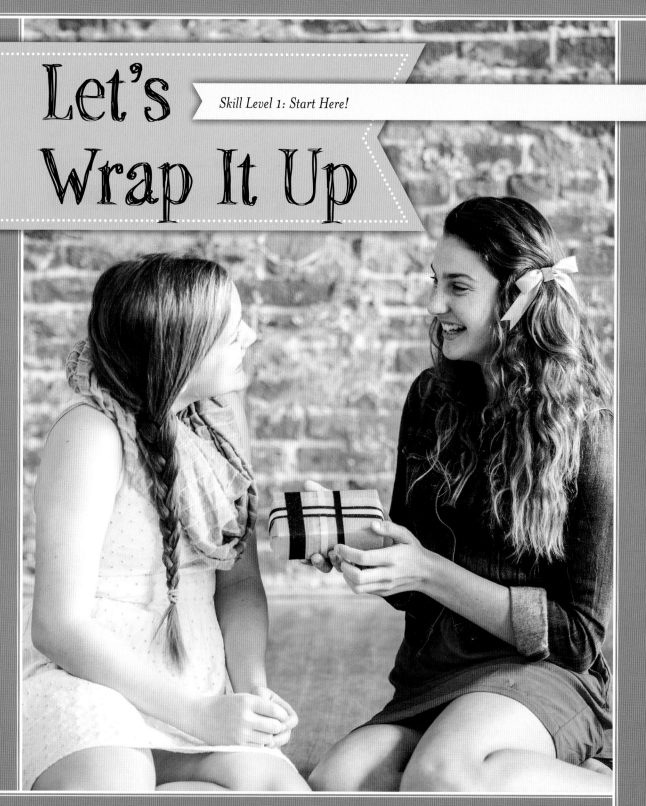

Let's Wrap It Up

Some of the greatest things in life are free! **Scour your house for some of those brown paper bags your parents are always folding up and tucking away** after grocery trips. After a little snipping and gluing, you'll have a low-cost (or no-cost!) way to make pretty packages for birthdays and holidays.

Make It Easy!

1. Wrap your present in Kraft paper and secure it with double-sided tape.

2. Measure *around* the package in both the long and short directions. Add ½˝ to each of these measurements. Cut 3 pieces of ribbon to wrap lengthwise (the longer side of the box) and 4 pieces to wrap widthwise (the shorter side).

3. Wrap the 4 widthwise ribbons around the box, overlap the ends, and use doubled-sided tape to hold them in place on the bottom side of your package.

4. Use the 3 other ribbon pieces to weave over and under the widthwise pieces, as shown. Overlap the ends and attach them to the bottom side of the box with double-sided tape.

Well, look at you! Turning a pretty present into a piece of art!

Make a special bow or ribbon to pop on top of your package. Your present will go from pretty to pretty exciting just like that! I used a Felt Wind-Up Flower (page 26) and leaves cut out with decorative-edged scissors.

Make It Fabulous!

Good-to-Know Glossary

Baker's Twine: This is a type of string that was originally used just to tie up packages from the bakery. Today, we use baker's twine as a decorative string for all kinds of crafty projects.

D-Rings: These metal rings are sold in pairs, and guess what, they are shaped like a letter D! They are great for making belts and for attaching handles to sewn projects.

Embroidery: This is a type of stitching that creates a raised design on fabric. You can embroider by hand (which is soooo fun!), but there are also special sewing machines that can embroider.

Embroidery Hoop: This is a set of two circles, with one hoop that fits inside the other. It is used to hold fabric taut for sewing that will show on the surface of the fabric, such as embroidery.

Embroidery Floss: This is a special kind of multistrand thread that is used for embroidery.

Fabric Stiffener: This is used to harden a piece of fabric, ribbon, or trim. Just dip the material in the stiffener. It will dry completely clear and will help your project to hold its shape.

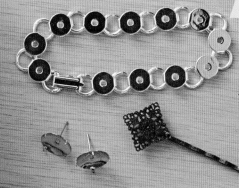

Findings: These are the components that you can use when making something like jewelry or accessories. Some examples of jewelry findings are earring backers, ring bases, bracelet blanks, and barrette blanks. You can glue embellishments to all of these.

Hot Glue Gun: This tool is perfect for many different crafts and projects because the glue dries quickly. But don't forget what makes it work: heat! I like to use a low-temperature glue gun because it gets warm enough to glue things together but is not quite as hot as a heavy-duty glue gun. Even a low-temperature glue gun can burn you, so always ask an adult before plugging in this tool. Make sure an adult is close by to help if you need it. Keep your glue gun on a plate or piece of cardboard while it is heating because sometimes it gets drippy!

Felt: This is a material made out of wool or acrylic fibers pressed together into a sheet. You can cut it with scissors and it won't fray. It comes in different thicknesses and colors.

Pinking Shears: These are scissors with a zigzag blade. This type of scissors is great because it keeps the edges of fabrics and ribbons from fraying! If you have a pair for cutting fabric, be sure not to use them for cutting paper. Otherwise the edges will dull really quickly!

Kraft Paper: This smooth, brown, very strong paper is meant for wrapping packages but also works great for many kinds of crafty projects.

Sequin: This is a small, shiny disc that can be sewn or glued to ribbon or clothing. Sequins also come stitched onto a string, which makes them really easy to use.

Interfacing: This is a material used between layers of fabric to give a project body and stiffness. Some interfacing is sewn into place, and some has a fusible (heat-activated glue) side, so it can be ironed right onto the fabric.

Find Good Stuff Here!

Craft Stores

If you have any of these craft stores near you, you'll be able to find pretty much *all* the supplies used in this book! If you don't live close to any of these, you can shop their online web stores with a parent's permission.

Michaels Stores

Jo-Ann Fabric and Craft Stores

Hobby Lobby

Also, check local listings or ask friends about **independent local shops** that might carry supplies you need. It's always nice to shop in your own neighborhood!

Other Fun Places to Check Out

Riley Blake does not have an online shop, but you can find retailers through its website. Riley Blake offers fabric and tons of gorgeous trims. Plus, their site is full of tips, ideas, and tutorials you are sure to love! • *rileyblakedesigns.com*

Cloud 9 Fabrics provided some fabrics for this book, and its website is full to the brim with beautiful fabrics and project ideas. Please do visit! • *cloud9fabrics.com*

And These, Too!

Dollar Store Crafts *dollarstorecrafts.com*

Spoonful Crafts *spoonful.com/create*

Molly Moo Crafts *mollymoocrafts.com*

About the Author

Maryellen Kim lives in Virginia with her little family. She and her husband, Dave, have a big garden, lots of flowers, three kids, and a very fuzzy cat. Her designs are a reflection of the joys in her life: family and the creative process.

Maryellen's studio is filled with tubes of paint, piles of fabric, bowls of beads, and jars of buttons. A self-proclaimed supply hoarder, Maryellen has never met a craft medium she didn't love. She finds inspiration everywhere and swears she'll someday find a use for that towering pile of magazines!

Her days are spent running Twist Style jewelry design and production studio; managing her brick-and-mortar storefront, Handmade Happiness Boutique; and teaching classes at The Happiness Factory, her open studio space for sharing skills and teaching classes. If she's not hanging out in the studio making stuff, she's probably at home eating chocolate chip cookies and crocheting!

Please visit her:

Facebook: Twist Style by Maryellen Kim
Twitter: @twiststyle
Instagram: twiststyle
Website: twiststyle.com